CANDLE

Day by Day

Bible

Presented to

....

By

....

On this day

....

**CANDLE
BOOKS**

Published by Candle Books
an imprint of
Lion Hudson plc
Wilkinson House, Jordan Hill Road,
Oxford OX2 8DR, England
www.lionhudson.com/candle

ISBN 978 1 85985 824 0
e-ISBN 978 1 78128 147 5

First edition 2014

Acknowledgments

Scripture quotations marked NLT are taken or adapted from
the Holy Bible, New Living Translation, copyright © 1996
by Tyndale House Foundation. Used by permission of Tyndale House Publishers, Inc., Carol Stream, Illinois 60188.
All rights reserved.

Scripture quotations marked REB are taken or adapted from
the Revised English Bible, copyright © Oxford University
Press and Cambridge University Press 1989. All rights
reserved.

Scripture quotations marked NJB are taken or adapted from
The New Jerusalem Bible, copyright © 1985 by Darton,
Longman & Todd Ltd. and Doubleday, a division of Random
House, Inc. Reproduced by permission. All rights reserved.

Scripture quotations marked CEV are taken or adapted from
the Contemporary English Version copyright © 1991, 1992,
1995 by American Bible Society. Used by permission.

Scripture quotations marked NRSV are taken or adapted
from the New Revised Standard Version Bible: Anglicized
Edition, copyright © 1989, 1995 National Council of the
Churches of Christ in the United States of America. Used by
permission. All rights reserved.

Scripture quotations marked KJV are taken or adapted
from The Authorized (King James) Version. Rights in the
Authorized Version in the United Kingdom are vested in the
Crown. Reproduced by permission of the Crown's patentee,
Cambridge University Press.

Scripture quotations marked NIV are taken or adapted from
the Holy Bible, New International Version® NIV® Copyright
© 1973, 1978, 1984 by Biblica, Inc.® Used by permission.
All rights reserved worldwide. The "NIV" and "New International Version" are trademarks registered in the United
States Patent and Trademark Office by Biblica, Inc.® Use of
either trademark requires the permission of Biblica, Inc.®

Scripture quotations marked NEB are taken or adapted from
the New English Bible, copyright © Oxford University
Press and Cambridge University Press 1961, 1970. All rights
reserved.

Scripture quotations marked GNB are taken or adapted from
the Good News Bible © 1994 published by the Bible Societ-
ies/HarperCollins Publishers Ltd UK, Good News Bible ©
American Bible Society 1966, 1971, 1976, 1992. Used with
permission.

A catalogue record for this book is available from the British Library

Printed and bound in Singapore, April 2014, LH01

CANDLE
Day by Day
Bible

by Juliet David
illustrated by Jane Heyes

CANDLE
BOOKS

OLD TESTAMENT

NEW TESTAMENT

OLD TESTAMENT

Can you guess what God did next?

In the beginning

In the very beginning, God made heaven and earth.
There were no people. No animals. No life at all.
And there was no light. It was dark. Very dark.
Completely dark.
And very empty.

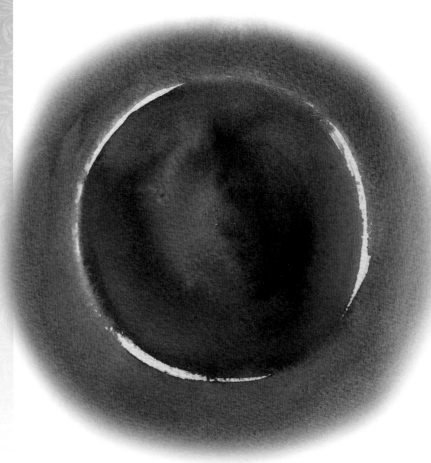

The first day

So on the first day God said, "Let there be light!"
    And there was light.
    God called the light "day" and the darkness "night".
    And God saw it was good.
    That was on day one!

Story
2

God said, "Let there be light."

Genesis 1:3 NLT

How many days did God take to create the world?

11

Sky, sea, and earth

God looked at what he had done and saw that it was good.

Genesis 1:10
CEV

On day two God put water in the sea and clouds in the sky.

God saw it was good.

Then on day three God made oceans, lakes, rivers, waterfalls, and streams.

He made dry land – mountains, hills, and valleys.

"Now let the earth turn green," said God. "Let grass, flowers, and trees grow. Let them have seeds and fruit!"

Lush grass, bright flowers, and tall trees started to grow on the earth. So many different kinds that nobody could count them all.

How many kinds of flowers and trees do you know?

Sun, moon, and stars

"There should be lights in the sky!" said God on day four. "They will divide time into hours, days, months, and years."

So God made spring and summer, harvest-time and winter.

He made the bright sun to warm the earth in the daytime.

God saw the night was very dark, so he put the moon and the stars in the sky. That night the moon and sparkly stars came out for the first time.

So day four's work was finished!

And it was all good.

God said,
"I command
lights to appear
in the sky."

Genesis 1:14
CEV

Do you ever
look up at the
night sky in
wonder?

Swimming and flying

*God gave the
living creatures
his blessing.*

Genesis 1:22 CEV

**Think how
many creatures
appeared on
day five!**

"Let there be living creatures in the water," God said on day five, "and in the air!"

So he made fish and all other creatures that swim: jellyfish, eels, sharks, whales, and turtles. Shellfish, flying fish, dolphins, crabs, and seahorses.

And God made birds and all other flying creatures. Eagles that soar, hawks that swoop, and hummingbirds that dart. Larks that sing and owls that hoot.

And God saw it was very good. That was day five!

Life on earth

God said, "Let
the earth bring
forth every
kind of animal."

Genesis 1:24 NLT

"Let there be life on the earth!" said God on day six.

So he created all the creatures that live on land.
Huge ones, such as elephants; and tiny ones, such
as mice. Handsome ones, such as tigers; and funny-
looking ones, such as anteaters. Some, like cheetahs,
could run fast; others, like turtles, moved so slowly.
And God made insects – some flying, some crawling,
and some jumpy.

God saw that it was all very good.

Can you think of anything on earth that was missing?

Humans

But God thought something was missing.

So he said, "Now I shall create humans!"

God took dust from the ground and formed it into a man's body.

He breathed into it, and the man came alive.

God named that first man Adam.

Adam was different from the animals, because he was like God.

God created
people in his
own image.

Genesis 1:27 NLT

*In what ways
are humans
different from
other animals?*

17

God said, "It
is not good for
the man to be
alone."

Genesis 2:18 NLT

**Why did God
create Eve?**

Adam and Eve

God knew it wasn't good for Adam to be the only person. Adam needed a companion.

So God made a woman from Adam's ribs.
Her name was Eve.

"Now start a family," God said to Adam.
"In time, let your family spread out all over
the earth!

It's also your job to care for the fish,
the birds, and all other
living creatures."

All finished

On the seventh day... God rested from all his work.

Genesis 2:2 NLT

Where do you think Adam and Eve lived?

So the earth and skies, plants, animals, and human beings were all created in six days.

God saw everything that he had made.

It was all very good!

And on day seven God rested.

He didn't make anything new.

"Now I've finished what had to be done," he said.

That's how God created the heavens and the earth.

In the garden

The man
named the
tame animals
and the birds
and the wild
animals.

Genesis 2:20 CEV

God gave Adam and Eve a beautiful garden to live in.
It was called the Garden of Eden.

"Now give names to all the animals I have created,"
God told them.

Adam and Eve had great fun, making up names
for all the living creatures! Alligators and caterpillars,
hippopotamuses and tortoises, squirrels and porpoises.

What do you think is the funniest animal name?

A special tree

The garden was full of wonderful fruit trees.

"Enjoy the garden!" God told Adam.
"You can eat anything you like."

But he gave Adam and Eve one warning:
"Never, ever eat the fruit from
that special tree in the middle
of the Garden of Eden," God
said. "That is the Tree of the
Knowledge of Good and Evil.
If you taste the fruit from that
tree, you will die."

Did they taste it?

*The Lord God
put the man in
the Garden of
Eden to take
care of it.*

Genesis 2:15 CEV

21

Peace in the garden

A river flowed
from the
land of Eden,
watering the
garden.

Genesis 2:10 NLT

*Can you
imagine what
life was like in
the Garden of
Eden?*

So Adam and Eve started to explore the garden.

They enjoyed the flowers and fruit, and they sat by the streams and lakes.

They walked through the trees and lay in the soft grass.

Adam and Eve looked after all the creatures that were living peaceably with them in the Garden of Eden.

*Now the
serpent was
more crafty
than any other
wild animal.*

Genesis 3:1 NRSV

The snake speaks

One day a sneaky snake slithered up to Eve.

"Sssssss," he sneered. "Why don't you steal a bite from the fruit on this tree?"

"No!" Eve replied. "We can eat from every tree except the Tree of the Knowledge of Good and Evil. God said if we eat *that* fruit, we will die."

"No, you won't!" the snake told her. "Just take a tiny bite. It can't hurt you. I'll tell you a secret: it will make you wise like God!"

So Eve took a bite of the fruit from the forbidden tree.

*Why do you think Eve ate
the fruit?*

Forbidden fruit

Before long Adam came to find Eve.
 "Here, taste this fruit!" she said to Adam.
"I've had a bite – and it hasn't harmed me at all."
 She gave some of the fruit to Adam.
 He too bit into the forbidden fruit.

What did God say about this?

The fruit looked so fresh and delicious, and it would make her so wise!

Genesis 3:6 NLT

25

Story
15

*They heard
the voice of
the Lord God
walking in the
garden in the
cool of the day.*

Genesis 3:8 KJV

This was to be
their last day in
the garden.

Blame

That afternoon God came walking in the
Garden of Eden.

Adam and Eve hid behind some trees.

"Adam! Eve! Where are you?" God called.
Soon he found them.

"Why were you hiding away from me?"
he asked them.

"I was afraid," Adam answered.

"Why?" God asked.

"Have you eaten the fruit I told
you not to eat?"

"Eve gave me some,"
said Adam, "and I ate it."

"The sneaky snake tricked
me," explained Eve, also
blaming someone else.
"That's why I ate the fruit."

Punished!

"Because you ate the fruit I told you not to eat," God said, "you will always have to work hard, growing crops. And one day you will both die."

God was very sad. Adam and Eve had not done as he had told them.

So God sent Adam and Eve out of the Garden of Eden. Forever.

He set angels with flashing swords to stop them from returning to the garden.

Never again would Adam and Eve see its beautiful flowers and trees, or enjoy quiet walks beside its rivers.

The Lord God banished Adam and his wife from the Garden of Eden.

Genesis 3:23 NLT

Why was God sad?

*"You are dust,
and to dust you
shall return."*

Genesis 3:19 NRSV

Outside the
garden, there
were thistles
and thorns,
nettles and
weeds.

Hard work

Adam and Eve felt very sorry and very sad.

Outside the garden, they worked so hard.

They had to grow their own food, sowing seeds, tearing up weeds, and tending plants.

Adam and Eve toiled day after day. Digging and sowing, hoeing and raking, weeding and watering.

Sometimes they thought of the happy times, when they still lived in the Garden of Eden.

Two sons

Eve had two sons, named Cain and Abel.

When they grew up, Cain became a farmer, and Abel became a shepherd.

The time came for each of them to offer God a special gift. Cain brought grain and fruit, and Abel gave a lamb. God was pleased with Abel's offering, but he didn't accept Cain's gifts.

"If you do well, will you not be accepted?"

Genesis 4:7 NRSV

Do you think Cain was happy about this?

29

The bad brother

Cain began to hate Abel, because God accepted Abel's gift, but not his.

One day, when they were in the fields, Cain attacked his brother Abel and killed him.

"Where is your brother?" God called to Cain later.

"How should I know?" Cain answered angrily. "Am I supposed to look after him?"

"You have killed your brother," said God. "Now you must leave home. You will wander all over the world. And your crops will never grow well."

Story 19

"Am I my brother's keeper?"

Genesis 4:9 KJV

Cain had to live in the Land of Wandering, east of Eden.

Things get bad

Before long, hundreds of people were living on earth.

But it became a bad place. People hurt one another. They stole from each other. They lied. They killed.

God kept warning them. But most people took no notice. God began to be sorry he had created the earth and its people.

"I will send a great flood," said God. "Water will cover the earth. It will drown every living thing: people, animals, snakes, birds, and insects."

The Lord was sorry that he had made humankind on the earth.

Genesis 6:6 *NRSV*

Would anyone survive?

One good man

*The Lord was
pleased with
Noah.*

Genesis 6:8 CEV

God saw that one good man was living on the earth.
His name was Noah.

God wanted to save Noah and his family from
the flood.

"I'm going to send a great flood," God told Noah.
"It will cover the whole earth with water. When the
flood is finished, I will give the
world a fresh start."

Noah felt worried.

"How can I save my family
from this terrible flood?"
he asked God.

*Why did God
choose to save
Noah from the
great flood?*

A plan

"I have made a plan to save you and your family,"
God told Noah. "You must build yourself a huge ship.
I will call it an 'ark'. It will be big enough for you,
your wife, your three sons – Shem, Ham, and Japheth
– and their wives too."

"I'll do exactly what you tell me," said Noah.

"The ark will also have room for the animals – at
least two of every kind – birds, reptiles, and insects,"
God explained to Noah.

God described to Noah exactly how to build
this great ark. How large it should be.
How many doors. How many windows.
How to make sure it didn't leak.

Noah was the
only person
who lived right
and obeyed
God.

Genesis 6:9 CEV

*What do you
think Noah's
friends said
when they saw
him building a
huge boat?*

Noah works hard

**Noah did
everything God
told him to do.**

Genesis 6:22
CEV

Noah started to build the ark. There was no time to lose. Noah's three sons all helped.

They cut down trees. They sawed up planks of wood. They hammered and smoothed and painted.

They worked for month after month, because this ship was to be the biggest ever built.

It was three floors high and had lots of big rooms inside. But it had just one door and one window.

Why do you think Noah was in a hurry to build the ark?

Two by two

Then God gave Noah his next instructions.

"Now collect up two of every kind of animal," he told Noah.

So Noah and his sons collected two of every creature on earth, one male and one female.

Two fierce lions, two howling tigers, two polar bears, two lumbering elephants, two scuttling lice, two cawing ravens, two cooing doves – even two spinning spiders, and two scarlet ants.

All of them would be safe from the flood that was coming.

Noah obeyed God and took a male and a female of each kind of animal... into the boat with him.

Genesis 7:8–9
CEV

God made sure that every sort of animal would survive the flood.

35

Into the ark

Story 25

When they were all in the boat, the Lord closed the door.

Genesis 7:16 CEV

What do you think happened next?

At last the ark was finished.

Then the weather changed suddenly. The skies grew dark. Thunder rumbled.

"The great flood is on its way!" Noah told his family. "It's time to enter the ark."

Noah opened the door of the ark and led in all the creatures. The fierce lions, howling tigers, lumbering elephants, scuttling lice, cawing ravens, cooing doves – even spinning spiders and scarlet ants.

"You must go in now too," God told Noah, "with your wife, your sons, and their wives."

So Noah and his family entered the great ark.

37

The sky opened like windows, and rain poured down.

Genesis 7:11 CEV

How long did it rain for?

Afloat!

The wind howled and the ark shook. Lightning flashed, thunder rumbled. Great drops of rain started to fall. Harder and harder it rained.

Slowly, the waters started to rise.

Before long, water covered all the land and everything living on it.

Finally the water lifted the ark off the earth.

They were floating!

All safe on board

The rain kept falling for more than a month.

But Noah and his family were safe inside their boat.

Gradually, they got used to hearing the rain beating on the roof of the ark and the thunder roaring.

And they were busy. The animals had to be fed and watered. There was so much to do.

At last the wind began to drop. Gradually, the rain stopped too.

The birds started to flutter their wings. Soon it would be safe to fly into the sky again.

Slowly, the waters went down.

God did not forget about Noah and the animals with him in the ark.

Genesis 8:1 CEV

How did Noah find out when it was safe to leave the ark?

39

*After forty
days, Noah
opened the
window he had
made in
the ark.*

Genesis 8:6 NIV

**How would
Noah know
that the water
had gone
down?**

Landing

Then one day the ark came to rest, with a roar and a crash. They had landed on the slopes of Mount Ararat.

But Noah and his family stayed inside the ark, waiting for God to tell them it was safe to come out.

"I'm going to send out a raven," Noah told his family one day.

The raven flew off – but never came back. It kept flying around and around until there was dry ground for it to land on.

Dove and leaf

Next Noah sent out a dove.

But the dove soon flew back: she could find nowhere to perch and rest.

So Noah waited about a week before he sent her out again. Once more she flew back to the ark.

But this time the little dove was carrying a fresh, green leaf in her beak.

Everyone smiled: it meant the tops of trees were now above water.

Story
29

The dove returned... holding in its beak a green leaf from an olive tree.

Genesis 8:11 CEV

How do you think Noah felt when the dove returned with a green leaf?

The door opens

Story
30

God said,
"Let out the
birds, animals,
and reptiles,
so they can...
live all over the
earth."

Genesis 8:17 CEV

When the
ground was
dry, God told
Noah it was
time to come
out of the ark.

After another week, Noah sent out the dove a third time. This time she never returned.

Soon the earth was dry enough to walk on again.

"Now it's time to leave the ark," God said.

The great door was opened. Noah, his family, and all the creatures left the ark.

The fierce lions, howling tigers, lumbering elephants, scuttling lice, cawing ravens, cooing doves, spinning spiders, and scarlet ants all came out of the ark.

The animals ran off to search for food. The birds flew away, high into the air.

The rainbow

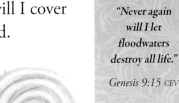

Noah and his family left the ark too.

Noah built an altar, where he could worship God.

He thanked God for saving them all from the flood.

"Even if people disobey me, never again will I cover the whole earth with a flood," God promised. "As long as the earth remains, there will be seed time and harvest, summer and winter. When it rains, look up at the sky. Sometimes you will see a beautiful rainbow. It will remind you of my promise."

God said, "Never again will I let floodwaters destroy all life."

Genesis 9:15 CEV

When was the last time you saw a rainbow?

*"Let's build
a city with
a tower that
reaches to
the sky!"*

Genesis 11:3 CEV

**What's the
tallest building
you know?**

A great tower

Noah's sons had
many children and
grandchildren.

They did many
things that made
God angry.

At that time,
everyone spoke the
same language.

Some people
decided to build
a huge tower that
would reach high
into the sky.

"This gigantic
tower will show just
how great we are!"
they boasted.

All mixed up!

God was angry when he saw the tower these people were building. They were much too pleased with themselves!

So God decided to stop them.

When the builders woke up one morning, they were all speaking different languages. Nobody could understand a word anyone else was saying!

So they couldn't work together. They had to leave the tower unfinished.

This tower was called "Babel" – which means "mixed up". The languages were mixed up – and so were the people!

The Lord confused their language and scattered them all over the earth.

Genesis 11:8 CEV

Do any of your friends speak a different language?

45

A fresh start

Long ago, in a far-off land called Ur, lived a man named Abram.

Abram was married to Sarah. They were both old, but they had no children.

One day God said to Abram, "Leave your home and your friends. Take a long journey with Sarah to a new country. I'm going to give you a special new land."

This country was Canaan. Because God promised it to Abram, we also call it the "Promised Land".

How would you feel about moving to a new country?

A mystery journey

Abram and Sarah were bold. They believed God, and they were ready to leave home.

With Abram's nephew, Lot, they started out for Canaan, taking their servants, their camels, their cattle, and their sheep.

Abram was rich; having many animals was like having lots of money.

Abram had no map for their journey. But God explained, "I will show you where to go – and how to reach the land I've promised you."

How did Abram and Sarah know where to go?

The Lord
promised,
*"I will give this
land to your
family forever."*

Genesis 12:7 CEV

A new land

Story 36

The Lord said to Abram, "Walk back and forth across the land, because I am going to give it to you."

Genesis 13:17
CEV

Abram and Sarah were already old. Was it easy for them to believe God's promise?

After journeying many months, Abram and Sarah came to the land that God had promised.

In the land of Canaan were lush, green valleys and fast-flowing rivers.

"This is the country I told you about!" God told Abram. "I'm giving this land to you, to your children, and to your grandchildren."

Abram thanked God for bringing him and his family to such a wonderful country.

And Abram always remembered God's promise, "One day you will have many children, grandchildren, and great-grandchildren.

Fighting for land

Abram had huge herds of camels and cows,
and great flocks of sheep and goats.

His nephew Lot had lots of animals too.

Their servants started to fight over the best land
for their animals.

So Abram said to Lot, "This is a big country.
Let's divide the land between us. You take first pick!"

Was Abram kind to Lot? In what way?

Abram said to
Lot, "We are
close relatives.
We shouldn't
argue."

Genesis 13:8 CEV

49

A selfish choice

Lot chose the best land, near the River Jordan, where there was plenty of water for his animals. He wanted to live in the nearby wicked city of Sodom.

Abram could have kept the best land for himself. But he was generous and let Lot choose.

After Lot moved away, God made more wonderful promises to Abram.

Captured!

About that time, four kings attacked the city of Sodom. They stole money, food, clothing, and jewels.

They even carried away some people from Sodom, including Lot.

When Abram heard Lot was in trouble, he gathered his servants and chased after the four kings' army.

They caught the kings and defeated them in a battle. Abram rescued his nephew Lot.

Although Lot had been greedy and taken the best land, Abram still wanted to help him.

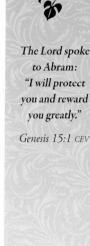

The Lord spoke to Abram: "I will protect you and reward you greatly."

Genesis 15:1 CEV

Abram complains

Abram believed the Lord, so the Lord was pleased with him and accepted him.

Genesis 15:6 CEV

Was this the first time God made this promise to Abram?

Sarah was by now too old to have children.
Abram was even older.

"We've been waiting years to start a family,"
Abram complained to God. "We'll both die
before we have any children!"

"Go outside your tent," God said to him that night.
"Now look up at the stars!"

Abram looked.

"Can you count them?" God asked.

Abram shook his head.

"You will have as many children, grandchildren,
and great-grandchildren as there are stars in
the night sky," God promised Abram.
"You wouldn't even be able to
count them."

Sarah gets impatient

But Sarah became impatient for a son.

"Take Hagar, my servant girl, as your second wife," she said to Abram. "Then we can have a baby in the family."

So Abram married Hagar, and Hagar had a baby boy.

He was named Ishmael.

Why do you think Sarah became impatient?

When Hagar knew she was going to have a baby, she became proud and treated Sarah hatefully.

Genesis 16:4 CEV

53

Abram's new name

It was Abram's birthday. He was ninety-nine years old!
For his birthday, God gave him a new name: "Abraham". It means "father of many".

"Remember the promises I made to you," God said to Abraham. "Every one of them will come true!"

What new name would you choose?

The Lord appeared to Abram again and said, "I am God All-Powerful."

Genesis 17:1 CEV

Three visitors

Not long after, Abraham was sitting in front of his tent one lunchtime. It was burning hot.

Suddenly, three men Abraham didn't know walked up.

"Come here and sit in the shade," Abraham called to them. "Then you can eat with me."

"Quick! Bake some bread!" Abraham told his wife.

"Prepare a feast!" he ordered his servant.

When lunch was ready, Abraham brought it out to his visitors.

The Lord appeared to Abraham near the great trees of Mamre.

Genesis 18:1 NIV

In Bible times, it was very rude for men to enter the women's part of the tent.

55

Sarah laughs

"Is anything too hard for the Lord?"

Genesis 18:14 NLT

Do you think God kept his promise to Abraham and Sarah?

After the meal, one stranger asked Abraham, "Where is your wife, Sarah?"

"Inside the tent," Abraham replied.

One of the three visitors was the Lord God.

"Next year Sarah will have a baby," he told Abraham. "A boy baby."

Sarah was listening through the wall of the tent. She laughed!

"I can't have a child at my age," she said to herself.

"Why did Sarah laugh?" the stranger asked Abraham. "*Nothing* is impossible for God."

Bargaining with God

When the three visitors were ready to leave, Abraham walked with them toward Sodom, where Lot lived.

"If the people of Sodom are doing wrong," said the Lord, "I am going to punish them."

Abraham didn't want Lot to be hurt.

"If there are fifty good people in Sodom," Abraham said to the Lord, "will you change your mind?"

"Yes," said the Lord.

"If there are forty good people in Sodom, will you change your mind?"

"Yes."

"If there are thirty?"

"Yes."

"If there are twenty?"

"Yes."

"If there are ten good people in Sodom, will you change your mind?"

And the Lord God answered, "Yes."

Then Abraham went home.

The Lord said, "I have chosen Abraham to teach his family to obey me forever and to do what is right and fair."

Genesis 18:19 CEV

Do you ever bargain with your dad the way Abraham bargained with God?

57

The angels' warning

*"Run for your
lives!" the
angels warned.*

Genesis 19:17 NLT

That evening two angels went to Sodom to warn Lot
that trouble was coming.

"Get out quickly!" they said. "God is going to
destroy this city. He can't find even ten good people
here."

So Lot, his wife, and their daughters left.

"Don't look back!" the angels warned.
"Run to the mountains and hide."

Lot's wife turned around to take a final look at her
home in Sodom.

At that very moment, she turned into
a pillar of salt!

But Lot and
his daughters
hurried on.

**What a
terrible thing
happened to
Lot's wife!**

Terrible fire

Lot and his daughters escaped.

But fire poured down on Sodom.

Everything burned up – the buildings, the animals, and the plants.

From far away, Abraham saw the smoke rising from those terrible fires.

Now he knew that the Lord could not find even ten good people in Sodom.

God remembered his promise to Abraham and saved Lot from the terrible destruction.

Genesis 19:29 CEV

Although Sodom was destroyed, Lot escaped.

More laughter

The Lord did exactly what he had promised.

Genesis 21:1 NLT

Almost a year after the three visitors came to Abraham's tent, Sarah had a baby boy – just as God had promised.

"God has made me so happy," said Sarah.

She named her baby Isaac, which means "laughter".

Did God keep his promise to Abraham and Sarah?

Ishmael goes away

When Isaac was a bit older, Abraham gave a big party for him. Abraham's older son, Ishmael, was there too, and started to tease Isaac.

Sarah was furious.

"Send Ishmael and his mother Hagar away!' she shouted at Abraham.

"Let them go," God said to Abraham. "I will look after them."

So Abraham gave Hagar and Ishmael food and water and then sent them off into the desert.

God said, "I will make Ishmael's descendants into a great nation."

Genesis 21:13 CEV

How did Hagar and Ishmael survive in the desert?

61

Water in the desert

*God was with
the boy as he
grew up in the
wilderness.*

Genesis 21:20 NLT

As Hagar and Ishmael walked on through the hot desert, they quickly ran out of water. Hagar was afraid her son Ishmael might die of thirst.

Ishmael lay down in the shade of a bush.

Hagar sat alone, crying.

"God has heard you," an angel told Hagar. "Go and look after your son."

As she walked back to Ishmael, Hagar noticed a well. She filled her water bottle from the well and gave Ishmael a drink.

God listened to Hagar's cry for help.

Soon the boy felt fit enough to continue the journey through the desert.

Isaac seeks a wife

Isaac grew up a fine young man. He helped his old father, Abraham, look after his flocks of sheep and herds of cattle.

Soon the time came for Isaac to get married. Abraham called for his servant, Eliezer.

"Go back to the land I first came from," Abraham told him. "There you must find a good wife for my son, Isaac."

So Eliezer loaded up his camels with gifts, and set out on a long journey to find a wife for Isaac.

Abraham was now a very old man, and the Lord had blessed him in every way.

Genesis 24:1 NLT

How would Eliezer know who God had chosen to marry Isaac?

63

*"I thank you,
Lord God of
my master
Abraham! You
have... kept
your promise to
him."*

Genesis 24:27 CEV

Thirsty camels

At last Eliezer arrived in the country that Abraham had journeyed from years before. Only then did he ask himself, "How will I find a wife for Isaac?"

"The woman who gives you water for your camels to drink will be Isaac's wife," God told him.

Just then a young woman came to the nearby well to fill her water pot.

"May I have a drink?" asked Eliezer.

"Yes, sir!" she replied. "And I'll gladly draw water for your camels too."

The woman kept drawing water until all the camels had had enough to drink. Eliezer knew this *must* be the woman God wanted to become Isaac's wife.

*Did Eliezer
think this
woman was
kind?*

A wife for Isaac

"What is your name?"
Abraham's servant asked the
young woman.

"Rebekah," she told him.
"Come home with me and
meet my family."

When they arrived at
Rebekah's home, Eliezer
took out the gifts he'd
brought and gave them to
her family.

"I am Abraham's servant,
from Canaan," Eliezer
explained. "I prayed that
God would show me a wife
for Isaac. I believe God has
chosen Rebekah. "

"We can see God brought
you here," said Rebekah's
father. "And I would be
very happy for my daughter
to marry Isaac."

*"The Lord
has obviously
brought you
here, so what
can we say?"*

Genesis 24:50 NLT

***Do you think
it's strange that
Isaac hadn't
met Rebekah
yet?***

Isaac loved
Rebekah very
much.

Genesis 24:67 NLT

Isaac and
Rebekah had
never met, so
now they got
to know each
other.

The bride arrives

Next morning Rebekah packed her things and set off with Eliezer for the Promised Land to meet Isaac.

They journeyed many days.

One evening, just before sunset, the camels halted. A young man was walking in the fields. When he looked up, he noticed the camels.

It was Isaac! He soon saw the beautiful young woman riding one of the camels.

His bride had come!

Rebekah prays

*Isaac asked
the Lord to let
Rebekah have
a child, and the
Lord answered
his prayer.*

Genesis 25:21 CEV

**God answered
Rebekah's
prayer.**

Isaac and Rebekah were quickly married.

They knew that, years before, God had promised Abraham, "One day you will have as many children, grandchildren, and great-grandchildren as there are stars in the night sky."

But at first Rebekah had no children.

Isaac and Rebekah prayed earnestly to God.

After that, it wasn't long before Rebekah was expecting twins.

Rebekah's first twin was covered in red hair – even when he was a baby. They named him Esau.

Jacob, the second twin, was quite different. He had soft, smooth skin.

Unalike twins

Story 56

Isaac loved Esau... but Rebekah loved Jacob.

Genesis 25:28
NRSV

As they grew up, the twin brothers became less and less similar to each other.

They looked different, they did different things, and they didn't even get along with one another.

Esau became a bold huntsman, killing wild deer for food.

Jacob was quieter and liked to stay at home. He was Rebekah's best-loved son. Jacob was always full of tricks and schemes.

Do you know any twins? How similar are they?

68

Jacob tricks Esau

One day Esau came home from hunting, tired and hungry. He saw Jacob was cooking broth.

"Give me some of that!" said Esau. "I'm starving!"

Jacob was soon up to his tricks.

"Give me your special rights as Isaac's oldest son," said Jacob, thinking quickly. "Then you can have as much broth as you want!"

"All right!" said Esau foolishly. "It's a bargain! I'd give anything for some food."

So Jacob gave Esau a bowl of steaming broth. Esau didn't even notice that his brother had tricked him.

He ate, drank, got up, and went away. That was all Esau cared about his birthright.

Genesis 25:34 NJB

Did Esau make a good decision?

69

Story 58

"Which one of my sons are you?" Isaac asked. Jacob replied, "I am Esau, your firstborn."

Genesis 27:18–19 CEV

Another trick!

By this time Isaac was very old and had lost his sight.

He wanted to give Esau his special blessing, as Isaac's eldest son. But Rebekah wanted Jacob to get this blessing.

While Esau was out hunting, Rebekah tied hairy bits of animal skin to Jacob's arms. Then Jacob went in to see his father, Isaac.

"Father, give me your special blessing," said Jacob, trying to make his voice sound deep, like Esau's.

Why do you think Rebekah tied animal skins on Jacob's arms?

Hairy arms

Old Isaac wasn't sure that it *was* Esau.

"Stretch out your arms," he said. "Let me feel your skin. If it's hairy, I'll know you really are Esau, my eldest son."

Jacob held out his arms, with the skins tied to them. Isaac touched the skins. They felt hairy – so Isaac thought it must be Esau.

Then Isaac gave Jacob his special blessing.

Isaac said, "The voice is the voice of Jacob, but the hands are the hands of Esau."

Genesis 27:22
NIV

Was it smart of Jacob to fool Isaac?

71

Jacob runs away

Isaac said, "May
God Almighty
bless you and
give you many
children."

Genesis 28:3 NLT

Soon after this, Esau returned from hunting.

When he discovered what Jacob had done, he was furious.

"Jacob has stolen my blessing!" he yelled. "I'll kill him for this!"

"Go and stay with my brother, Laban, until Esau calms down," Rebekah told Jacob. "I'll let you know when it's safe to come home."

So Jacob ran away to his uncle Laban.

Did Jacob's trick turn out well for him?

A wonderful dream

One night, while he was on the run,
Jacob went to sleep alone in the desert.
He used a big rock as his pillow.

Jacob had a wonderful dream.
He saw a stairway to heaven,
with angels walking up
and down.

"I am the God of
Abraham and Isaac,"
said a voice. "You will
have many children
– and this land will
be yours forever."

*The Lord said,
"Wherever you
go, I will watch
over you."*

Genesis 28:15 CEV

**God made a
promise like
this to someone
else. Who was
that?**

73

House of God

Jacob woke up, both excited and afraid, because God had spoken to him in a dream.

He named this place Bethel, which means "house of God".

Then he set off again on his journey.

After many weeks, Jacob reached his uncle Laban's house. For the time being, he was safe from his angry brother, Esau.

Jacob thought, "The Lord is in this place, and I didn't even know it."

Genesis 28:16
CEV

Why did Jacob call this place "House of God"?

Jacob in love

Laban had two daughters, Leah and Rachel.

Before long, Jacob fell in love with Rachel, Laban's younger daughter. He wanted to marry her.

Uncle Laban told Jacob, "If you work for me for seven years, you may marry my daughter."

So Jacob stayed seven long years. He worked hard every day, so that he could marry Rachel, the woman he loved.

Jacob worked for seven years for Rachel, and they seemed to him like a few days, because he loved her so much.

Genesis 29:20
NJB

Is there something you would wait seven years for?

Story
64

"Why did you trick me?" Jacob asked Laban.

Genesis 29:25
CEV

How do you think Jacob felt when he realized he'd been tricked?

Jacob gets a shock

Finally the time came for Jacob's wedding.
His bride wore a veil that hid her face.
Then Jacob received a terrible shock!
When his bride took off her veil, Jacob discovered
that he had married Leah.
Laban had tricked Jacob.
He had given Jacob his
older daughter, Leah –
not Rachel.

Jacob's reward

Jacob was very angry indeed.

"What have you done to me?" he shouted.

"Work for me seven years more – *then* I'll give you Rachel as your wife," said Laban.

Jacob loved Rachel so much that he worked seven more years for Laban.

Then at last Jacob married his beloved Rachel.

Story
65

Jacob loved Rachel more than he did Leah.

Genesis 29:31
CEV

Now how did Jacob feel?

77

Jacob goes home

Story
66

*Jacob said,
"When I left
home, I owned
nothing except
a walking stick,
and now my
household fills
two camps!"*

Genesis 32:10
NLT

*What do you
think happened
when the
brothers met
again?*

After many years living with Laban's family, Jacob decided it was time to go home. He took his flocks and left while Laban was away shearing sheep.

When Jacob had almost reached home, a servant warned him, "Your brother Esau is coming out to meet you!"

Jacob felt frightened.

Perhaps Esau was still angry with him.

"God save me from my brother!" he prayed.

78

Friends at last!

Next morning Esau arrived at Jacob's camp.

Jacob knelt before him fearfully.

But Esau ran to Jacob and hugged him! He was overjoyed to see his brother Jacob again, after all these years.

"Tell me, Jacob," asked Esau, "who are all these people journeying with you?"

"My wives, Leah and Rachel," Jacob answered, "my children, my servants, and my flocks and herds. God has given me so many good things."

And after this, the quarrelsome brothers lived peacefully as friends!

Jacob said, "God has been very generous to me. I have more than enough."

Genesis 33:11
NLT

How sad it was that Isaac wasn't alive to see his sons become friends again.

79

Story 68

Joseph's coat

By the time he returned from his uncle Laban's house, Jacob had a big family.

He had twelve sons – and he loved every one of them dearly.

But Jacob loved his young son Joseph more than all the rest.

One day Jacob gave Joseph a fantastic coat.

How smart he looked! But it made his brothers very jealous.

Why should Joseph always get the best presents?

One day Jacob gave Joseph a special gift – a beautiful robe.

Genesis 37:3 NLT

Do you sometimes feel jealous of your brother or sister?

Joseph the dreamer

Joseph's brothers hated him more than ever because of what he had said about his dream.

Genesis 37:8 CEV

Sometimes Joseph had strange dreams.

"I've had a very odd dream," he told his brothers one morning. "We were in the fields at harvest time. All of us had bundles of grain. But then your bundles bowed down to my bundle."

Joseph's brothers were furious.

"So you think we should all bow down to you?" asked one.

"You're not king over us!" said another.

What do you think the brothers thought the bundles of grain stood for?

Another dream

Later Joseph had another peculiar dream.

"I dreamed that the sun, the moon, and eleven stars were bowing down to me," he told his family.

This time Jacob was angry with him.

"Do you really think your mother and I, and your brothers, should bow to you – like the sun, moon, and stars in your dream?" he asked furiously.

By now Joseph's brothers really hated him.

Joseph's father kept wondering about the dream.

Genesis 37:11 CEV

What did Joseph's brothers do next?

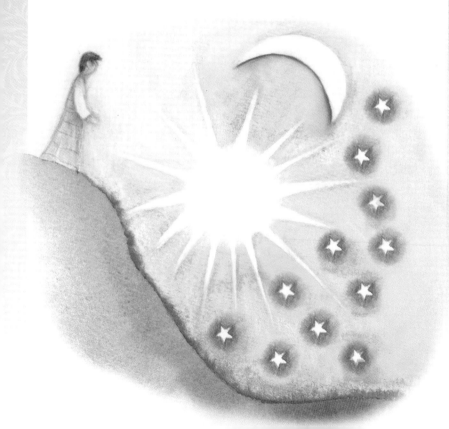

Story
71

*"Here comes
that dreamer!"
exclaimed
Joseph's
brothers.*

Genesis 37:19 NLT

**Why did
Joseph's
brothers hate
him so much?**

Joseph and his brothers

"Your brothers have taken my sheep to graze a day's
journey away," Jacob told Joseph one day.
"Go and take some food to them."

So Joseph set out with food for his brothers.

While he was still a long way off, Joseph's brothers
saw him coming.

"Now let's get rid of Joseph!" said one brother.

"Yes – this is our big chance!" agreed another.

Reuben's plan

But Joseph's oldest brother, Reuben, hated the idea of killing his brother.

"Let's leave him down this dried-up well," he said. "He'll die there anyway."

The others agreed with his plan. But Reuben actually planned to rescue Joseph later.

So when Joseph arrived, his brothers grabbed him, ripped off his coat, and threw him down the well.

"We must not take his life," said Reuben.

Genesis 37:21
NJB

Poor Joseph! What will happen to him now?

85

The brothers sold Joseph... for twenty shekels of silver.

Genesis 37:28
NJB

Sold as a slave

While Reuben was away, his brothers saw some traders riding past on camels.

"I've got a great idea!" said one. "Let's sell Joseph to those traders."

"Great thinking!" said another.

So the brothers hauled Joseph out of the well and sold him to the merchants.

The traders journeyed on toward the land of Egypt, taking poor Joseph with them.

How terrible – to sell your own brother!

Jacob weeps

By the time Reuben reappeared,
Joseph had gone.

"What are we going to say
to Father?" he asked.

They decided to pretend
Joseph had been eaten
by a wild animal. They
killed a goat and
splashed its blood on
Joseph's coat. Then
they went home.

"We found this by
the road," they said
to Jacob, handing
him the torn coat.
"He must have been
attacked by some
wild animal."

No one could
comfort Jacob.
He believed his
best-loved son
had died.

*"I will die in
mourning for
my son," Jacob
would say.*

*Genesis 37:35
NLT*

**Would Jacob
ever see Joseph
again?**

Joseph in Egypt

*The Lord was
with Joseph
and blessed
him greatly.*

Genesis 39:2 NLT

Meanwhile the traders arrived in Egypt with Joseph.
They took him to the marketplace.

A rich Egyptian named Potiphar bought Joseph,
and took him to work in his house.

Joseph thought he'd never see his own home again.
But he worked hard for Potiphar, and did everything
he was asked to do.

Soon Potiphar put Joseph in charge of his house.

God was still
looking after
Joseph.

Lies!

Joseph was quite happy for a time.

But before long came more trouble.

Potiphar's wife came to dislike Joseph, so she lied to her husband.

"Joseph attacked me," she told him.

Potiphar was so angry that he had Joseph thrown into jail.

While Joseph was in prison, the Lord helped him and was good to him.

Genesis 39:20–21
CEV

Potiphar treated Joseph unfairly. But God had a plan.

Prison dreams

*Joseph said,
"Doesn't God
know the
meaning of
dreams?"*

Genesis 40:8
CEV

God helped
Joseph to
understand
dreams.

Even in prison, people came to trust Joseph.

Before long, the jailer put Joseph in charge there.

The king's cup-bearer and the king's baker were
in the same jail. One night each of these men had a
strange dream. They recounted their dreams to Joseph,
and God helped him to explain them.

"The meaning of your dream is this," Joseph told
the cup-bearer. "In three days, Pharaoh, king of Egypt,
will send for you. You will stand beside him once
again, serving his wine."

Joseph helps

Then Joseph spoke to the baker.

"I'm very sorry," he said. "Your dream means that, in three days, Pharaoh will have you put to death."

Everything happened just as Joseph said.

"Remember me, when you stand beside Pharaoh!" Joseph said as the cup-bearer left prison. "I don't want to spend the rest of my life here."

But the cup-bearer soon forgot all about Joseph.

Everything happened just as Joseph had said it would.

Genesis 40:22
CEV

Did Joseph spend his life in prison?

91

Pharaoh dreams

One night Pharaoh, king of Egypt, had strange dreams.

He described his dreams to his wise men.

"In my first dream," said Pharaoh, "I was standing by the river, when seven fat cows came out of the water. Then came seven skinny cows – and they gobbled up the seven fat ones."

The king was upset. So he called in his magicians and wise men and told them what he had dreamed.

Genesis 41:8
CEV

Do you sometimes have scary dreams?

92

Not such wise men

"Now tell us your second dream, O Pharaoh," said the wise men.

"In my other dream, I saw seven good ears of grain growing. Then seven bad ears gobbled up the good ears of grain," said Pharaoh. "Whatever do my dreams mean?"

The wise men thought hard.

"We have no idea!" they confessed finally.

So Pharaoh sent them all away.

None of them could tell Pharaoh what the dreams meant.

Genesis 41:8
CEV

What do you think Pharaoh's dreams meant?

Send for Joseph!

"Joseph told us what each of our dreams meant, and everything happened just as he said it would."

Genesis 41:12–13
NLT

At that very moment, the king's cup-bearer remembered his friend Joseph.

"In your prison," the cup-bearer told Pharaoh, "there is a young man who explains dreams. He once explained an extraordinary dream of mine."

"Send for him at once!" ordered Pharaoh.

And in no time at all, Joseph was standing before Pharaoh.

God was carrying out his plan for Joseph.

What does it mean?

"First I will describe my dreams," Pharaoh told Joseph. "Then you must tell me what they mean."

"I can't do that!" said Joseph.

Pharaoh glowered at him.

"You see, it's *God* who tells me the meaning of dreams," Joseph explained.

"God can give a good meaning to your dreams," Joseph answered.

Genesis 41:16
CEV

Can you remember someone who had a special dream in the desert?

God has shown
you what he
intends to do.

Genesis 41:28
CEV

Joseph explains

So Pharaoh retold his dreams, and Joseph listened carefully. When Pharaoh had finished, Joseph prayed to God. Then he spoke.

"O Pharaoh! Your two dreams mean exactly the same thing," he explained. "The seven fat cows are seven years with plentiful harvests. The seven skinny cows are seven bad years with no harvest. The seven good ears of grain are also seven years of plenty," he went on.

"The seven poor ears of grain are seven hungry years."

*Who helped
Joseph
understand
Pharaoh's
dreams?*

Nothing to eat

"God has sent these dreams to warn you," Joseph explained to Pharaoh. "For seven years, everyone will have plenty to eat. But for the following seven years there will be no harvest, and nothing to eat."

Pharaoh looked very worried.

"How can I keep my people from starving in those bad years?" he asked. "I must look after my people."

God has definitely decided to do this and... he will do it soon.

Genesis 41:32
CEV

What did Pharaoh do to help his people?

97

Storehouses

*Who did
Pharaoh
choose to
help him?*

"O mighty Pharaoh, you need to find a very wise person," said Joseph. "This person must save up some of the grain from each of the seven good years."

Joseph thought hard, then he continued.

"You need to build storehouses. Save the grain in these storehouses until the seven bad years come – then open up the storehouses and sell the grain. In this way, people will have grain to make bread to eat."

Joseph the wise

"You've solved all my problems, Joseph," said Pharaoh.
"You understood my dreams – and then explained
how I can help my people. You shall become my chief
minister!"

For seven years, Joseph worked hard for Pharaoh.
He saved part of the grain each year and put it in
storehouses. When the seven hungry years came, he
opened up the storehouses and sold the grain.

So the people of Egypt had enough to eat, even
during the worst years of famine.

*Pharaoh said,
"Who could do
it better than
Joseph?"*

Genesis 41:38
NLT

God used
Joseph to help
the people of
Egypt.

Pharaoh said,
"Since God
has revealed
the meaning of
the dreams to
you, you are the
wisest man in
the land!"

Genesis 41:39
NLT

*What do
you think
Joseph felt
when he saw
his brothers
again?*

The brothers visit

Jacob and his family were still living in Canaan.
When the seven bad years came, they couldn't get
enough bread.

"Go to Egypt and buy grain," Jacob told his sons.

So ten brothers set off for Egypt to find food. The
youngest, Benjamin, stayed home with his old father.

When Joseph saw his brothers coming for grain, he
recognized them straight away.
But they didn't recognize him.
They bowed low to him
– just as in his dreams,
years before.

Grain in Egypt

"You've all come to spy on Egypt," Joseph said sternly to his brothers, to test them.

"No!" they said. "We've come simply to buy food. Our family in Canaan is very hungry."

Joseph gave them grain.

"If you come back to Egypt for more grain," he said, "you must bring your youngest brother too."

Do you think Jacob was happy for Benjamin to go to Egypt?

Jacob said to his sons, "I have heard there is grain in Egypt. Go down and buy some for us before we all starve to death."

Genesis 42:2
NLT

Together again!

*Although
Joseph
recognized
his brothers,
they did not
recognize him.*

Genesis 42:8
NIV

*Why was
Joseph
particularly
happy to see
Benjamin?*

The brothers took their sacks of grain back to Canaan.
But before long, they needed more.

So the brothers returned to Egypt, this time taking
young Benjamin.

"Prepare a feast for these brothers,"
Joseph ordered.

Joseph came to the feast.
He was so happy to see
his brother Benjamin
again!

Joseph gave his
brothers all the grain
they wanted.

Joseph's trick

Now Joseph played a trick on his brothers. He hid a silver cup inside Benjamin's sack of grain.

Then Joseph shouted, "My precious silver cup's gone! Someone has stolen it."

"Search all the sacks," Joseph ordered.

Soon his guards found the missing cup hidden in Benjamin's sack.

"Benjamin cannot return home with you," Joseph said sternly.

Judah [Joseph's brother] said, "God is punishing us for our sins."

Genesis 44:16
NLT

This is what the brothers feared most.

103

*"I am Joseph,
your brother,
whom you sold
into Egypt."*

Genesis 45:4 NLT

Joseph tested
his brothers:
they were
much kinder
than before.

Changed men

"Please don't keep Benjamin here in Egypt!" begged Joseph's brothers, weeping. "It will kill our old father, Jacob."

Then Joseph saw that his brothers had grown kinder, and loved their father dearly. He started to weep too.

"I am your brother Joseph!" he told them finally. "Now hurry home, tell Father the good news, and bring him here."

Israelites

Old Jacob was amazed when he heard his sons' story!

Now Jacob, his sons, and their families journeyed to Egypt. How glad Jacob was to see his beloved son Joseph again!

Joseph presented his father to Pharaoh, who welcomed him kindly. Jacob's family now made their home in Egypt.

Jacob was given a new name, "Israel". The Bible calls his family and their descendants "Israelites". A later name for them is the "Jews".

God said to Jacob, "I will go with you down to Egypt, and I will bring your descendants back again."

Genesis 46:3–4
NLT

Sometimes the Israelites are called "children of Israel".

Cruel Egyptians

After Jacob died, the Israelites kept growing in number. As years went by, his children, grandchildren, and great-grandchildren became so numerous that no one could count them. Many years before, God had promised Abraham this would happen: now it had!

The Pharaoh now ruling Egypt knew nothing about Joseph. But he was worried about how many Israelites were living in his land. He thought they might become so strong that they would turn against him.

So he told his people, the Egyptians, to make the Israelites work hard for them as slaves.

*Why was this
Pharaoh so
worried about
the Israelites?*

106

A baby in a basket

Still the Israelite families grew.

Then Pharaoh gave a terrible order. "Throw every Israelite baby boy into the River Nile!" he said. "No more Israelite men will grow up in my land."

An Israelite mother named Jochebed had a baby boy. She was frightened soldiers would snatch him away, so she made a plan.

She set to work with her daughter, Miriam, making a basket from reeds.

When it was ready, she said, "Now put baby in!"

Then they hurried to the river and floated the basket on the water.

Miriam hid in the rushes to keep watch.

Pharaoh gave all his people this command: "Throw every newborn boy into the river."

Exodus 1:22
NJB

Did Jochebed make a good plan for her baby?

107

The princess bathes

The child was crying, and Pharaoh's daughter was filled with pity for it.

Exodus 2:6 NEB

It was a great idea of Miriam's to ask her mother to care for the baby.

Before long, the princess of Egypt came to bathe in the river. She saw the basket and sent her maid to fetch it. When she looked inside, she was amazed to see a beautiful baby!

"I'm going to raise him as my own," she said.

At that moment, Miriam came out from hiding.

"Would you like me to find a nurse for him?" Miriam asked.

"Please do!" said the princess – and Miriam ran home and fetched her mother.

So Jochebed took care of her own little boy until he was old enough to live with the princess.

Story
96

The princess
named him
Moses,
"Because," she
said, "I drew
him out of the
water."

Exodus 2:10
NRSV

God made
Moses a prince
of Egypt.
But there
were bigger
surprises
ahead!

Prince of Egypt

The day came when Jochebed took her little boy
to live in the palace.

The princess named him "Moses".

After this, Moses was brought up as a prince
of Egypt.

But Moses never forgot that he was the son of
an Israelite slave. He felt very sorry for his people,
working so hard, making bricks in the hot sun.

"One day," thought Moses, "I must rescue my people."

Moses flees

When he was a little older, Moses went walking one
day near the mud-pits, where Israelites made bricks
for Pharaoh. He saw an Egyptian cruelly beating an
Israelite worker. Moses was so angry that he struck the
Egyptian dead.

Immediately Moses felt frightened. He had to escape
before Egyptian soldiers caught him!

Now what would happen to Moses?

**Moses fled
from Pharaoh
and went to live
in Midian.**

Exodus 2:15
NIV

Moses the shepherd

The Israelites cried out for help, and God heard their loud cries.

Exodus 2:23–24
CEV

Moses fled Egypt, escaping to the land of Midian.

One time he helped some Midianite women to get water from a well for their father's sheep. Their father was grateful to Moses and let him work as a shepherd for him.

Perhaps Moses wondered if he would ever return to Egypt.

Moses used to take the sheep out into the lonely desert. He led his sheep to water, scared away any wild animals, and protected his flock at night.

It was so different from life as a prince of Egypt.

The bush that burned

One day, as Moses was leading his sheep through the hot desert, he approached a great mountain called Sinai.

Nearby he noticed a bush on fire. But there was something strange! The bush burned and burned – yet it never burned away.

"How extraordinary!" Moses thought. "Why doesn't this bush burn away?"

Suddenly, he heard a voice calling, "Moses! Moses!"

"Here I am!" Moses answered.

"Why isn't that bush burning up? I must go over to see this."

Exodus 3:3
NLT

Can you think why the bush was burning like this?

113

Story
100

"I am the God of your father, the God of Abraham, the God of Isaac, and the God of Jacob."

Exodus 3:6 NIV

Why do you think Moses didn't want to do what God asked him to do?

God speaks

"Come no nearer!" ordered the solemn voice. "Take off your sandals. The place where you're standing is holy… I, God, am speaking!"

Moses was now trembling. He listened very carefully.

"I have seen how cruelly the Egyptians are treating my people, the Israelites," God told Moses. "I am going to help them. You must go to Pharaoh and tell him to let my people go free. Then you will lead my people out of Egypt."

"What, me?" said Moses, who was very fearful. "I can't possibly do that! No!"

"I will help you," God promised.

Moses' rod

Moses was still scared.

So God showed Moses just how powerful he was.

"Throw down your shepherd's rod," God said.

Moses did so – and the rod turned into a live snake. Moses jumped away.

"Grab the snake by its tail!" said God.

Carefully, Moses picked up the snake.

Immediately it turned back into a rod again.

"When I help you do that miracle," God told Moses, "people will believe I sent you."

God said to Moses, "I am who I am."

Exodus 3:14
NRSV

Why did God show Moses this miracle?

115

A helper for Moses

The Lord said,
"Who makes
people able to
speak?"

Exodus 4:11
CEV

God gave
Moses
someone to
help him –
his brother.

But Moses was *still* scared.

"I'm no good at speaking in public," he said.

"I never know what to say… I stutter and stammer."

"When you speak, Moses, I will give you the words to say," God promised.

"Lord, please send someone else – not me!" pleaded Moses.

By now, God was getting quite angry!

"Your brother, Aaron, is a good speaker," said God.

"Tell Aaron what to say – then *he* can do the talking for you."

At last Moses agreed to do the job that God wanted him to do.

At Pharaoh's palace

So Moses left his sheep and returned to Egypt.

With his brother Aaron, he marched boldly up to Pharaoh's palace.

Together they stood before the king of Egypt.

God gave Moses the words to say, and Moses passed them on to Aaron.

"O mighty Pharaoh!" said Aaron. "It is wrong to make people work as slaves." He paused. "The God of Israel says: 'Let my people go into the desert so that they can worship me!'"

"I don't know this God of yours!" shouted Pharaoh. "He can't tell *me* what to do. I will never let my Israelite workers go free!"

"The God of Israel says, 'Let my people go.'"

Exodus 5:1
NIV

Would Moses now give up trying to free his people?

117

No straw!

*"I am the Lord!
And with my
mighty power I
will punish the
Egyptians."*

Exodus 6:6 CEV

Pharaoh was furious that Moses and Aaron had dared to come to his palace telling him what to do.

He called in his captains.

"Force my Israelite slaves to work harder," ordered Pharaoh. "No longer give them straw for making the bricks. They must make as many bricks as before – but find their own straw too. They'll be so busy they won't have time to think about trips to the desert!"

So Pharaoh's captains made life still harder for the Israelites.

Perhaps Moses had made a mistake in coming to Pharaoh?

Moses complains

"I will bring you into the land that I solemnly promised to Abraham."

Exodus 6:8 CEV

What a terrible life for Moses' people, the Israelites!

The Israelite slaves worked hard in the blazing sun. If they slowed down, cruel Egyptians beat them.

The Israelites blamed Moses for their troubles.

"Everything has got worse since you asked Pharaoh to let us go," they moaned.

"I thought you were going to rescue my people," Moses complained to God. "But they're suffering even more than before you sent me to Pharaoh."

"Go back to Pharaoh!" God told Moses. "If he doesn't let my people go, Egypt will suffer terribly."

Story
106

Moses and Aaron did just as God had commanded them.

Exodus 7:6 NLT

What was God showing Pharaoh when Aaron's snake gobbled up the other snakes?

A gobbling snake

Moses and Aaron returned to Pharaoh's palace.

"Throw down your rod," God told Aaron.

Aaron did so – and at once his rod turned into a wriggling snake.

Pharaoh's magicians copied him and threw down their rods. They turned into snakes too!

But then Aaron's snake gobbled up all the other snakes.

Yet *still* Pharaoh did not let the Israelite slaves go.

Hard times

Now God sent some very hard times on Egypt.

Moses and Aaron entered Pharaoh's palace again.

"The God of Israel says: 'Let my people go!'" said Aaron.

"Do you think I'm going to do what *your* God says?" Pharaoh answered. "Forget it! I need Israelites to make my bricks and build my palaces. Now get out and stop bothering me!"

"If you disobey God," Moses warned, "he will turn the water of the River Nile to blood."

"I will not let your people go!" Pharaoh repeated.

Pharaoh's heart became hard and he would not listen.

Exodus 7:13 NIV

Do you think Pharaoh changed his mind after this?

Story
108

River of blood

So God turned the water of the Nile to blood.
No one could drink it. The fish all died.

Moses and Aaron went to the palace yet again.

"Ask your God to turn the blood back to water,"
Pharaoh pleaded. "When he does, I will let your
people go."

So Moses prayed, "Lord, please turn the blood in
the river back to water."

And God did as Moses asked.

But *still* Pharaoh did not let the Israelites go.

*The Lord says,
"By this you
will know that
I am the Lord."*

Exodus 7:17 NIV

Sometimes
people just
don't want to
listen to God –
like Pharaoh.

Frogs, frogs, frogs

Moses and Aaron returned to Pharaoh's
palace again.

"Let my people go!" said Aaron.
"If you don't, God will send a
plague of frogs all across your
land."

"I will not let your people go!"
said Pharaoh.

So God sent frogs into his
palace – and all over his land.

Pharaoh called for Moses.

"Get your God to take away the frogs,"
said Pharaoh. "Then I will let your people go."

Moses prayed, "Lord God, please will you take
away all these frogs."

The frogs went.

But *still* Pharaoh did not
let the Israelites go.

*"Everyone will
discover that
there is no god
like the Lord."*

Exodus 8:10
CEV

*How much
worse would
things get
before Pharaoh
changed his
mind?*

Gnats!

"God has done
this."

Exodus 8:19 CEV

**Which of these
"plagues" do
you think
was the most
unpleasant?**

Moses and Aaron returned to the palace again.

"Let my people go," said Moses. "If you don't,
God will send swarms of gnats right across Egypt."

"I will not let your people go," said Pharaoh.

So God sent swarms of gnats all over the land.
Pharaoh called quickly for Moses.

"Ask your God to take away the gnats," he requested.
"Then I will let your people go."

So Moses prayed, "Lord, take away all these
swarms of gnats!"

And the gnats vanished.

But *still* Pharaoh did not let
the Israelites go.

Flies!

Moses and Aaron went to the palace yet again.

"Let my people go," said Moses. "If you refuse, God will send swarms of flies all over your land."

"I will not let your people go," said Pharaoh.

So God sent swarms of flies right across Egypt. Pharaoh soon called for Moses.

"Ask your God to take away all these flies," he said. "Then I will let your people go – just a short distance."

Moses prayed, "Lord, please take away these flies!"

And the flies vanished.

But *still* Pharaoh did not let the Israelites go.

Moses prayed, and the Lord answered his prayer.

Exodus 8:30 CEV

What would it take to change Pharaoh's mind?

125

Story
112

*Pharaoh still
refused to let
the people go.*

Exodus 9:7
NLT

Sick animals

Moses and Aaron returned to the palace yet again.

"Let my people go!" said Moses. "Otherwise God will make every living creature in your land fall sick."

"I will not let your people go," said Pharaoh.

So God made all the animals fall sick.

In desperation, Pharaoh called for Moses.

"Ask your God to make the animals well again," he said. "Then I really will let your people go."

So Moses asked God to make the animals well again.

But *still* Pharaoh did not let the Israelites go.

***Why do you
think Pharaoh
kept on
changing his
mind?***

Sores and boils

Next painful boils and sores appeared on the skin of the Egyptians.

Then giant-sized hailstones fell on the fields.

Locusts – like grasshoppers – appeared in countless swarms. They ate every leaf on every tree, and every ear on every stalk of grain.

Next thick darkness came right across the land of Egypt. No one could see a thing!

Yet *still* Pharaoh did not let the Israelites go.

The Lord hardened Pharaoh's heart.

Exodus 9:12

NIV

What might make Pharaoh decide to let the Israelites leave Egypt?

127

The worst thing

"There will be loud wailing throughout Egypt."

Exodus 11:6
NIV

God said to Moses, "I am sending one last, dreadful punishment. After that, Pharaoh will beg you to go."

So Moses went before Pharaoh a final time.

"During the night, the eldest son in every Egyptian family is going to die," Moses told Pharaoh. "After that, you will plead with the Israelites to leave your country. Then I will take my people and go."

Moses turned and hurried out of the palace.

Now Moses had to prepare his people to leave Egypt fast.

128

Lamb's blood

God gave Moses special instructions for that night.

"Tell the Israelites to kill a lamb and mark their doorways with the lamb's blood," he said. "I will go through the land, killing the sons of the Egyptians. Where I see blood over the door, I will pass over – and not kill your sons."

That night the Israelites marked their doorways with lamb's blood, and ate a special meal of lamb, as God had told Moses. They ate, wearing their outdoor clothes and holding their walking sticks.

Ever after, the Israelites remembered this night every year, at a festival they called "Passover". It reminded them that God had saved them.

"This is a day you are to commemorate."

Exodus 12:14
NIV

Do you know a Jewish family who celebrate Passover?

Go!

That terrible night the eldest son in every Egyptian family died. Even Pharaoh's son died.

Before it was even light, Pharaoh summoned Moses to his palace.

"Get your people out of Egypt!" he told Moses. "Hurry! Otherwise we will *all* fall sick and die."

Pharaoh said, "Up! Leave my people, you and the Israelites!"

Exodus 12:31
NIV

Was this the last Moses and the Israelites heard of Pharaoh?

Night-time escape

It was still the middle of the night.

Every Israelite family hurriedly packed everything they owned.

Then the Israelites left quietly, taking with them their flocks and herds. They didn't want the Egyptians to hear them leaving.

The people of Israel had started their long journey to Canaan, the Promised Land.

That very day the Lord began to lead the people of Israel out of Egypt.

Exodus 12:51
NLT

God loved his people and took care of them on their journey.

131

On the march

Pharaoh said,
"We have let
the Israelites go
and have lost
their services!"

Exodus 14:5
NIV

The Israelites walked day and night to escape from Pharaoh.

But when the Egyptians awoke to find that the Israelites had left, they were very angry.

"Who will work for us now?" they demanded. "Who will make our bricks and build our palaces?"

So Pharaoh changed his mind yet again. "Harness the horses to your chariots! Chase down those Israelites and drag them back to Egypt," he ordered his soldiers.

The Israelites faced great danger from Pharaoh and his army!

No way ahead!

Soon the Israelites had reached the shore of the Red
Sea. There they stopped. How could they cross the
deep waters of the Red Sea?

Suddenly, the Israelites saw clouds of dust and heard
pounding hooves. It was Pharaoh with his army! The
Egyptians were speeding up in their chariots, coming
to fetch the Israelites back to Egypt.

"What can we do?" the Israelites demanded. "The
Red Sea is in front of us – and Pharaoh and his army
are behind us. We will all die here, for sure!"

*"Don't be
afraid. Just
stand where
you are and
watch the Lord
rescue you."*

Exodus 14:13
NLT

*How do you
think the
Israelites felt
now?*

133

A path through the sea

The Lord opened up a path through the water.

Exodus 14:21
NLT

Then God gave Moses special instructions.

"Stretch out your hand!" he told Moses.

Moses stretched out his hand.

At once a strong wind blew a dry path through the Red Sea, and the waters divided.

The Israelites began to walk on dry land across the seabed. It wasn't long before they had all safely reached the opposite side.

How do you think it felt, walking on dry land across the sea?

135

Free at last

*"The Lord is
my strength,
the reason
for my song,
because he has
saved me."*

Exodus 15:2 CEV

Pharaoh's soldiers were still chasing after the Israelites, and soon arrived at the shores of the Red Sea. The Egyptians raced right on, between the great walls of water. But their wheels got stuck in the mud and started to fall off their chariots.

As soon as the last Israelite was safely across, Moses raised his hand again. The wind dropped, and the water flooded back onto the seabed.

Pharaoh, his chariots, and his soldiers all drowned. At last the Israelites were free.

The Israelites
thanked God
for rescuing
them from
Pharaoh and
the Egyptians.

Water to drink

But the Israelites still had a long, long way to go. They trudged on through the hot desert. Everyone grew thirsty; their tongues were dry and their skin scorched.

For three days the Israelites searched for water. At last they found a well and drew up water. *Yeeuchh!* It tasted so bitter they couldn't drink it.

"Do you want us to die of thirst here?" they asked Moses angrily. "We might as well have stayed in Egypt. At least we had water to drink there!"

Then God showed Moses a bit of wood lying on the ground. Moses threw it down the well.

The Israelites drew more water from the well. Now it tasted sweet! Everyone drank as much as they wanted.

"I am the Lord, who heals you."

Exodus 15:26
NIV

God looked after the Israelites in many different ways.

137

Food from heaven

The Lord said to Moses, "I will rain down bread from heaven for you."

Exodus 16:4
NIV

What did the Israelites see when they woke up the next day?

Before long, the Israelites ran out of bread. Everyone started to feel faint with hunger.

"Why did you ever lead us into this horrible desert?" they demanded angrily. "We will all starve to death here! We might as well have stayed in Egypt! At least we had enough to eat there!"

"You won't die," Moses told them. "God will take care of you. Just wait till morning – then you'll find something quite wonderful!"

Daily bread

Sure enough, when the Israelites woke in the morning, they discovered that the ground was covered with a strange, white powder. One man put some on his finger and licked it. It tasted sweet – and good! Soon they were all eating this new food.

The Israelites called it "manna". It appeared every morning – except on the Sabbath – the entire time the Israelites were journeying to Canaan.

"You will know that I am the Lord your God."

Exodus 16:12
NLT

We often pray, "Give us today our daily bread..."

Water from a rock

Soon the people ran out of water again.

"It's your fault," they complained to Moses. "You brought us out of Egypt to this dry desert. Now we're all going to die of thirst."

"Go to the rock that I show you," God told Moses. "Then take your rod and hit the rock. Immediately water will pour out."

Moses did just as God told him – and water flowed from the rock.

There was plenty for everyone.

War!

Soon the Israelites reached a place called Rephidim.

There an enemy army attacked them.

Moses chose a brave soldier called Joshua to lead the Israelite army.

"I will stand on a hill and watch," said Moses. "I'll hold up my rod. As long as I hold it out, God will help us to win."

Who would win the battle?

"I carried you on eagles' wings and brought you to myself."

Exodus 19:4 NIV

141

*"The Lord
Gives Me
Victory."*

Exodus 17:15
CEV

Moses said the
Israelites won
because he
depended on
God.

Victory!

While Moses held up his rod, the people of Israel were winning. But after a time, his arms grew tired and he had to lower the rod. Then the enemy started to win the battle.

Two friends found a big rock for old Moses to sit on. They stood each side of him and held up Moses' arms, so that his rod was always pointing over the battlefield.

At last the battle finished – and the Israelites had won!

Mount Sinai

The Israelites trudged on through the hot desert, week after week.

At last they reached the Desert of Sinai. Towering above the bare desert was Mount Sinai.

The mountain was so high that its peak was often hidden in clouds.

This was the very place where Moses had seen the burning bush, many years before.

Can you guess what Moses did next?

There, facing the mountain, Israel pitched camp.

Exodus 19:2

NJB

Moses on the mountain

Moses decided to climb the mountain alone, to meet with God.

When Moses reached the summit, God made a promise to Moses and to the people of Israel.

"I will be your God," he said, "and you shall be my people. You must live in a way that is pleasing to me."

"I am going to give you my rules for living," God then told Moses. "You must write them out on big, flat stones."

"I am the Lord your God, who brought you out of Egypt."

Exodus 20:2
NIV

What rules do you have in your school? What are they for?

Rules for living

So Moses wrote God's special rules for living on two slabs of rock.

We call these rules the "Ten Commandments":

1. *Do not worship any God except me.*
2. *Do not worship idols.*
3. *Do not disrespect my name.*
4. *You have six days when you can work;*
   the seventh, the Sabbath, is a day of rest.

"Do not worship any god except me."

Exodus 20:3
CEV

Can you remember the first day of rest? Look back to page 19.

145

Pleasing God

The rest of the commandments are about how we
should behave toward other people:

> 5. *Respect your father and your mother.*
> 6. *Do not kill.*
> 7. *Be faithful to your husband or wife.*
> 8. *Do not steal.*
> 9. *Do not tell lies about other people.*
> 10. *Do not wish for anything that belongs
>   to someone else.*

***Why do you
think God gave
these rules?***

A golden calf

Moses was away so long on Mount Sinai that many of the Israelites thought he wasn't coming back.

"Something must have happened to Moses," they told Aaron. "Make us a god who will take care of us."

So Aaron told them to bring him their gold rings, bracelets, and earrings. Then he melted them all down and formed a golden calf.

Aaron set up this calf in the middle of the Israelite camp. People started to bow down to it and dance around it. They forgot about the God who had brought them out of Egypt. Instead they began to worship the calf that Aaron had made from gold rings and bracelets.

The people said... "This is the god who brought us out of Egypt!"

Exodus 32:4
CEV

What would Moses say when he got back?

147

Moses is angry

The Lord said
to Moses,
"Hurry back
down! Those
people you led
out of Egypt
are acting like
fools."

Exodus 32:7
CEV

*Why was Moses
so angry?*

At last Moses came down Mount Sinai.

As he clambered down the steep mountain, he heard singing and shouting. He couldn't think what the noise was all about.

When he got a little further down, Moses saw the golden calf. He felt so angry that he threw to the ground the great stones with God's rules written on them. They smashed into lots of tiny pieces.

Then Moses stormed into the Israelite camp and smashed up the golden calf.

A shining face

The Israelites saw how angry they had made God. They told him they were very sorry for making the golden calf.

Moses had to climb Mount Sinai a second time, to get a new set of stones with God's rules on them.

God now also explained to Moses how the Israelites should worship, and how the special festivals were to be celebrated.

This time, when Moses came down the mountain, his face was shining, because he had been with God.

The Lord said, "I will go with you and give you peace."

Exodus 33:14
CEV

The Israelites were frightened when they saw Moses' shining face. Why?

"Come, all of you who are gifted craftsmen. Construct everything that the Lord has commanded."

Exodus 35:10
NLT

The Israelites were living in tents – so they made a big tent for God.

A very big tent

God also told Moses, "Build a huge tent where the people can pray." In the Bible this is often called the "tabernacle".

God described to Moses what furniture should go in the tabernacle: "Most important is the 'ark of the covenant': a beautiful wooden box, completely covered with gold. There will also be a golden lampstand with seven lamps, and altars on which the priests will make offerings."

Building God's tent

Story

136

"It's time to start building the tabernacle," Moses told his people. "Everyone can help by bringing things to help build and furnish it."

The Israelites gave Moses their earrings, bracelets, and precious jewels – the very best of what they owned. Everyone wanted God's house of worship to be as beautiful as possible.

Soon the great tent was completed. There was a special curtained-off room inside, called the "Holiest Place". The ark of the covenant was kept there. Only the high priest could go into this room, just once a year.

Inside the ark, Moses placed the stones on which the Ten Commandments were written.

When the Israelites moved on, they could pack up the tabernacle tent and take it with them.

And so at last the tabernacle was finished.

Exodus 39:32
NLT

Why do you think Moses put the Ten Commandments inside the tabernacle tent?

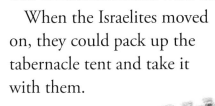

Set apart as
holy to the
Lord.

Exodus 39:30
NLT

Aaron the high priest

God put Moses' brother Aaron and his family in charge of the tabernacle. Aaron was the high priest, and his four sons all helped him. It was the priests' job to sacrifice the animals that the Israelites offered to God in thanks.

The priests wore special clothes. Aaron had an embroidered robe, covered by a blue coat. Around its hem were little bells. Over the coat, Aaron wore a vest with twelve different jewels sewn on the front. Each jewel stood for one of the twelve tribes of Israel.

Did you know that most of the tribes of Israel were named after the sons of Jacob?

Holy days

God told Moses, "The Israelites shall hold special festivals each year." There were three particularly important holidays.

Passover was the festival when the Israelites remembered how God passed over their homes in Egypt, and helped them escape from Pharaoh.

After they had gathered all their crops in, the Israelites thanked God at their **Harvest** festival.

At their **Tabernacles** festival, the Israelites remembered how they lived in tents as they journeyed to the Promised Land. For one week they lived in huts made from tree branches.

At each of these festivals, the people brought gifts of fruit or animals to the tabernacle.

Also, every week the Israelites had their Sabbath, a day when they rested and prayed to God. They remembered how God rested after creating the world.

The Lord told Moses... "I have chosen certain times for you to come together and worship me."

Leviticus 23:1–2
CEV

Which is the Christian day of rest?

153

Moving on

The Israelites spent some time at Mount Sinai.

"Now journey on to the land I promised you," God told them. "Remember, I will always be with you."

So the people packed up their tents, left Mount Sinai, and moved on. The journey was long and dangerous, and they had many adventures.

Often they grumbled and complained. Sometimes they disobeyed God.

But God never gave up on them.

When they stopped to set up camp, Moses would pray, "Our Lord, stay close to Israel's thousands and thousands of people."

Numbers 10:36
CEV

They were God's people: he never stopped loving them.

Checking out the land

"Send twelve men into Canaan to find out what it's like," God told Moses one day. "Tell them to bring back any fruit they find in the Promised Land."

So Moses sent off twelve spies to explore Canaan. Weeks later they returned, carrying luscious grapes, pomegranates, and figs.

"It's a beautiful land," said ten of them. "But the people of Canaan are fierce giants! We'll never drive them out."

However two spies – Caleb and Joshua – said, "It's a wonderful country. We should march right in!"

"God will lead us into this country and give it to us. It is a country flowing with milk and honey."

Numbers 14:8
NJB

Why did Moses send spies into the Promised Land?

155

More complaints

*The Lord said,
"You sinful
people have
complained
against me too
many times!"*

Numbers 14:27
CEV

The Israelites heard the ten spies telling Moses,
"The people of Canaan are fierce giants!"

They started to moan again.

"If only we'd stayed in Egypt!" they complained.
"Let's choose a new leader who'll take us back there."

God was angry: the Israelites didn't trust him. So
he made the Israelites wander around in the desert for
forty years more, instead of going straight to Canaan.

Did Moses reach the Promised Land?
Let's find out.

On Mount Nebo

After forty long years, Moses finally led the Israelites to another mountain, called Mount Nebo.

From the top of the mountain, they could see into Canaan, the land that God had promised them.

But Moses died on Mount Nebo, before he could enter the Promised Land. He was 120 years old. He had brought his people from Egypt right to the borders of Canaan.

"The Lord himself goes before you and will be with you; he will never leave you nor forsake you."

Deuteronomy 31:8 NIV

Poor old Moses! He never entered the Promised Land.

Joshua the leader

Now God made Joshua the leader of the Israelites.

"Prepare the people to cross the River Jordan," God told Joshua. "Don't be afraid! I will be with you and take care of you."

So Joshua told his people to get ready to cross the river and enter the Promised Land.

How would the Israelites cross the river?

Moses said
to Joshua,
"Be strong and
courageous,
for you must
go with this
people into the
land."

*Deuteronomy
31:7 NIV*

Rahab hides spies

Joshua sent two spies ahead, to find out about the city of Jericho, just across the river. In Jericho, the spies stayed at the home of a woman named Rahab.

The king of Jericho heard there were spies in his city and sent soldiers to search for them. Rahab hid the two men on the roof of her house.

When the soldiers arrived, she said, "The Israelite spies have just gone! Hurry – you might catch them before they leave the city!"

*Rahab said,
"I know that
the Lord has
given this land
to you."*

Joshua 2:9 NIV

God used a
woman from
Jericho to help
the Israelite
spies.

A red rope

Rahab went to find the spies, hiding on the roof.

"I know your God will help you defeat Jericho," she said. "Please save me and my family, because we helped you today."

"Hang a red rope out of the window – and stay inside with your family," they told her. "When we capture the city, we'll see the rope and know it marks your house."

Then the spies returned safely to the Israelite camp.

Do you think God did save Rahab and all her family?

Crossing the river

Joshua gathered his people on the edge of the river.
But how were they going to get across the river? There
were no bridges – and the water was running fast.

"Walk into the Jordan," God told the priests,
"carrying the ark of the covenant on your shoulders!"

The priests did so – and God cleared a dry path
through the water. The Israelites followed the priests
across to the opposite side of the river. Once they were
all safely over, the waters flooded back.

At last God's people had arrived in the Promised Land!

*"The Israelites
crossed the
Jordan on dry
ground."*

Joshua 4:22 NLT

Now that the
Israelites had
arrived in
the Promised
Land, God
stopped
sending them
manna every
morning.

A mighty city

The first place the Israelites came to was the great, old city of Jericho. It had high, thick walls and mighty gates. Watchful guards were posted everywhere.

The gates were all shut tight against the Israelites. No one could leave or enter. So the Israelites set up camp outside the city walls.

Next they celebrated the festival of Passover. They remembered how God had set them free from slavery in Egypt years before, in the time of Moses.

Why was it good to remember how God had brought them out of Egypt?

Joshua meets a stranger

Joshua was puzzling out how to capture Jericho. Suddenly, a man appeared, holding a sword.

"Are you for us – or for our enemies?" asked Joshua.

"I am the commander of the Lord's army!" the man replied.

Then God explained to Joshua how to take Jericho. "Each day, for six days, march your people around the city walls – seven priests in front, followed by the men carrying the ark of the covenant.

"On the seventh day march around the city seven times. Then tell the priests to blow their trumpets, and everyone else to shout. If you do all this, the walls will fall – and Jericho will be yours!"

"I am here because I am the commander of the Lord's army."

Joshua 5:14 CEV

What do you think the Israelites said when Joshua gave them these strange instructions?

The Lord was
with Joshua,
and his
fame spread
throughout the
land.

Joshua 6:27 NIV

When the
Israelites beat
Jericho, other
people living in
the Promised
Land got
scared.

Jericho falls

Each day, the Israelites went out and marched around the walls of Jericho, just as God had told Joshua.

The people of Jericho watched, very puzzled. What ever were the Israelites up to?

On the seventh day, the Israelites marched around the great walls seven times, following the priests and the ark of the covenant as usual.

The seventh time, the priests blasted on their trumpets, and every Israelite shouted at the top of his or her voice. What a noise!

Down crashed the walls, as God had promised. Before long, the Israelites had captured the whole city. Joshua remembered to take care of Rahab and her family, as he had promised.

Story
150

The Lord told
Joshua, "Don't
be afraid,
and don't be
discouraged."

Joshua 8:1 CEV

Israel defeated

This was just the first of many battles in Canaan.
Next Joshua had to conquer the nearby city of Ai.

"There are only a few soldiers there," Joshua's spies
told him. "We don't need a big army to take it."

Joshua sent off three thousand soldiers to capture Ai.
But the army of Ai beat them easily.

"Why didn't we win?" Joshua asked.

"Someone stole some gold from Jericho," God told
him. "I will show you the thief."

It was a man named Achan.

"I stole silver and gold, and hid
it in my tent," he said sadly.

One man
spoiled
things for the
Israelites.

166

Hidden treasure!

Joshua's men searched Achan's tent. There they found the gold and silver, buried in the ground.

"What you have done has brought defeat to our army," Joshua told Achan.

Now Joshua attacked Ai again. This time he hid thirty thousand soldiers behind the city, while the rest attacked from the front. When the army of Ai came out to fight, the thirty thousand Israelites hiding behind Ai came out and set the city on fire.

The people said to Joshua, "We will serve the Lord our God and obey him."

Joshua 24:24
NIV

Although Achan had done wrong, God continued to help his people.

167

*The Israelites
did what was
evil in the sight
of the Lord,
forgetting the
Lord their God.*

Judges 3:7 NRSV

One of the
"judges" of
Israel was a
woman named
Deborah.

Judges for Israel

With Joshua as leader, the Israelites gradually conquered the entire country. Now the Promised Land was their land.

But when Joshua died, some of the Israelites began to worship the gods of the people of Canaan. God saw this and sent enemy armies to defeat the Israelites. The Israelites told God that they were sorry, and that they would trust him again.

This happened time after time. Each time God forgave his people and gave them a strong leader to help them. These leaders were called "judges".

God chooses Gideon

One time, people called the Midianites were attacking God's people. "Help us!" prayed the Israelites. So God found them a new leader.

A man named Gideon was threshing grain one day when an angel appeared.

"God is with you, bold hero!" said the angel.

"I'm no hero. I'm just a farm worker!" Gideon answered. "And if God is on our side, why does he let the Midianites bully us?""

"God will help you rescue your people," said the angel.

"The Lord is peace."

Judges 6:24 NIV

God chooses all kinds of people to help him – not just the brave and the clever.

Story
154

The Lord said, "Go down into the Midianite camp, for I have given you victory over them!"

Judges 7:9 NLT

Why did God tell Gideon he needed only a tiny army to beat the enemy?

A shrinking army

Gideon called together thousands of Israelite men to help fight the Midianites.

"Send away anyone who's scared of fighting," God told him. So thousands of men slunk off home.

"You still have too many soldiers," God told him. "Go down with them to the stream. Take into battle anyone who scoops up water to drink in their hands."

Just three hundred soldiers drank the water this way.

"I'll help you beat the Midianites with this tiny army," God promised Gideon.

Surprise attack!

Gideon gave each soldier a trumpet, and a jar with a lighted lamp inside.

"When we get to the Midianites' camp," he explained, "we'll blow the trumpets, break the pitchers, and shout: 'The sword of God and of Gideon!'"

That night they attacked the Midianites. On a signal, Gideon's men broke their pitchers and shouted. The lights flared, and the noise was deafening.

The Midianites woke up, terrified. They thought a huge army was attacking – and fled.

Israel was free of the cruel Midianites!

Gideon said, "The Lord will rule over you."

Judges 8:23 NIV

With God's help, his people beat the Midianites.

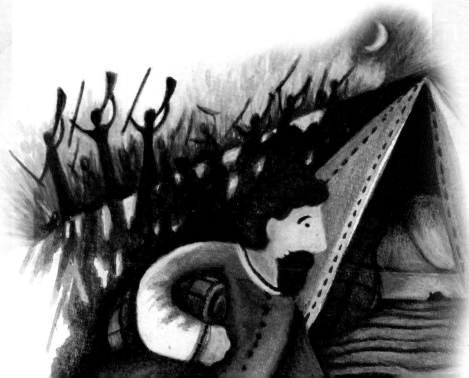

Samson the strong

As the boy grew, the Lord blessed him.

Judges 13:24 CEV

Soon the Israelites forgot about their God yet again. So God allowed the fierce Philistines to attack Israel.

God sent an angel to an Israelite man one day.

"Your wife is going to have a baby son," the angel told him. "He will have a special task. When he grows up, he will protect your people from the Philistines."

The boy was born, and his parents named him Samson. They never, ever cut his hair. They allowed it to grow really long, to show he was someone with a special job to do for God.

Can you think of someone else whose birth was foretold by an angel?

Samson's adventures

One summer Samson saw the Philistines' fields, ripe with grain. He grabbed some foxes, set light to their tails, and let them run free in the fields. Soon the Philistines' crops were ablaze: that year they had no harvest!

Another time Samson was attacked by a thousand Philistines. He picked up a donkey's jawbone and started hitting them. Soon he'd beaten the whole bunch of Philistines!

Samson always got the better of his enemies. He always won, he always managed to escape. He was just *too* strong for the Philistines.

The Spirit of the Lord came upon Samson in power.

Judges 14:19 NIV

Samson was very strong – but he wasn't always very smart.

173

Catching Samson

"*Samson, what makes you so strong?*"

Judges 16:6 CEV

The Philistines desperately wanted to catch Samson. But how could they, when he was so very strong?

At last they got a chance. Samson fell in love with a beautiful Philistine girl, named Delilah.

When they heard, the Philistine kings told Delilah, "We'll give you lots of money if you can get Samson to tell you what makes him *so* strong."

Delilah agreed.

Samson was foolish to choose Delilah as his friend.

174

Samson's secret

Next time she saw Samson, Delilah asked, "What makes you so strong, dearest?"

But each time Delilah asked him to explain his secret, Samson made up some story.

"If you tie me up with new bowstrings," he told her, "I'll be no stronger than anyone else."

She tried this – but Samson snapped the strings as if they were strands of wool.

Another time he told Delilah, "Tie me with a brand new rope – then my strength will disappear!"

She tried this too – but Samson broke the rope as if it were a thread of cotton.

The third time she asked, Samson said, "Weave my hair in a loom – then I'll be as weak as a baby."

Delilah tried this too – but Samson easily yanked his hair out of the loom.

Delilah said, "You've made me look like a fool three times."

Judges 16:15
CEV

Will Delilah discover Samson's secret?

175

Samson is shaved

Samson finally told her the truth. *"I have belonged to God ever since I was born."*

Judges 16:17 CEV

Poor Samson! He must have felt very sorry he had trusted Delilah.

"If you won't tell me what makes you so strong," Delilah complained, "it will show you don't love me."

She sulked and whined, until finally Samson gave in.

"If someone completely shaved my head," he whispered to Delilah, "I'd lose all my strength. I'm strong because of my long hair."

That night, as soon as he fell asleep, Delilah cut Samson's hair. *Snip, snip, snip!*

In that moment, Samson lost all his strength. Philistine soldiers burst in, tied him up, and dragged him off to jail. Samson had no strength to resist them.

A guest in chains

Months later the Philistines threw a party for their god, Dagon.

"Let's bring Samson here!" shouted someone. "We can all have a laugh at the strong man. He's so weak now!"

So guards marched Samson from prison to the temple where the party was being held.

The Philistines jeered at him.

"Aren't you supposed to be so strong?" they mocked. "How come you're in chains?"

What had they forgotten?

Samson's
strength was
gone.

Judges 16:19
CEV

177

Samson's last victory

*Samson called
to the Lord
and said,
"Lord God,
remember me
and strengthen
me."*

*Judges 16:28
NRSV*

But while he'd been in prison, Samson's hair had started to grow. The Philistines hadn't noticed! By now his hair was quite long again.

Samson heard the Philistines mocking him.

"Lord, give me back my old strength!" he prayed.

God answered his prayer.

Samson pushed with all his might against the pillars of the building. The pillars tipped. The walls fell. The roof collapsed!

Every Philistine inside the temple was killed. So was Samson. It was his final great feat of strength.

***Who made
Samson so
strong?***

179

*Ruth said,
"Your people
shall be my
people, and
your God my
God."*

Ruth 1:16 NRSV

**How did Ruth
show that she
loved Naomi?**

Naomi comes home

There was famine in the land, so one Israelite took his wife, Naomi, to the land of Moab, to find food. After a while, he died. When his sons grew up, they married Moabite women, named Orpah and Ruth. But both the sons died too.

When Naomi heard that the famine in Israel had finished, she decided to return home. Her daughter-in-law, Ruth, wanted to accompany her.

"I want to be with you and your people," said Ruth.

So they journeyed together to Naomi's home town, Bethlehem.

Ruth in the fields

Naomi and Ruth arrived in Bethlehem at the beginning of harvest.

They needed food, so Ruth went to the fields to pick up grain that the reapers had missed. The law said that dropped grain should be left for the poor.

Ruth was working in the fields of a rich farmer named Boaz. When he heard Ruth had been looking after her mother-in-law, Naomi, he wanted to help her.

"Please come every day and take all the grain you need," he said.

Before long, Boaz came to love Ruth.

Soon they married and had a little boy.

Boaz said to Ruth, "May... the God of Israel, under whose wings you have come to take refuge, reward you fully."

Ruth 2:12 NLT

God took care of Ruth when she was in another country.

Story 165

A good man

"Job is a truly good person."

Job 1:8 CEV

Poor Job! He didn't know what terrible things would happen to him.

Job was a very rich man.

He had a wife, seven sons, three daughters, and huge flocks and herds.

Job loved God and tried to please him.

"Job obeys you only because you have made him rich and given him a lovely family," Satan said to God.

"All right," God replied. "You test him. See what he does if you take some of those things away from him."

So Satan sent terrible troubles to Job.

Job is tested

First thieves stole Job's donkeys and oxen.

Then fire burned up his sheep and his shepherds.

Tribesmen ran off with Job's camels and killed his herdsmen.

A tornado destroyed the house of Job's son, with all his children inside.

Job was heartbroken.

"God gave me everything," he said. "Now God has taken it all away. But I *still* love him."

Satan hadn't yet finished.

"Job loves you because he's still healthy," said Satan.

So God told Satan, "You may even make Job ill."

And soon Job had horrible sores all over his body.

*Job did not sin
or accuse God
of doing wrong.*

Job 1:22 CEV

*Do you think Job
turned his back
on God?*

183

Job said,
"If God has
something
against me, let
him speak up!"

Job 31:35 CEV

***Did Job's
friends bring
him any
comfort?***

Job's friends

Now Job felt very sorry for himself.
Three friends visited. Job told them
everything that had happened.

"These troubles must be a punishment for
disobeying God," they agreed.

"But I've done nothing wrong," said Job angrily.
"I've always tried to live well and to please God."

At last Job got fed up with all his troubles. He
complained that God wasn't being fair with him.

God blesses Job

"Let me ask you a question, Job," said God. "Do you understand everything I created? Never forget: you are just a man – and I am Lord of the universe!"

"I know how wonderful you are," Job answered. "I'm very sorry I complained."

Then God gave Job back his health – and more riches than he had before. God even gave Job and his wife seven more sons and three more daughters – the same number as before.

The Lord said to Job, "Were you there when I laid the foundation of the earth?"

Job 38:4 NRSV

Even when bad things happen, God doesn't forget us.

Jonah runs away

"Say to the
people of
Nineveh,
'The Lord
has seen
your terrible
sins. You are
doomed!'"

Jonah 1:2 CEV

One day God spoke to an Israelite named Jonah.

"Go to the great city of Nineveh!" God told him. "Tell the people they are doing very bad things. If they don't change their ways, I'm going to punish them."

"I don't want to go telling people God's going to punish them," Jonah thought. "That's far too scary!"

So Jonah ran away instead. He headed for the coast and boarded a ship.

What happened next in Jonah's adventure story?

A great storm

*Jonah said,
"I worship...
the God of
heaven, who
made the sea
and the dry
land."*

Jonah 1:9 NRSV

**Did God hear
Jonah's prayer?**

Once they were at sea, God sent a terrible storm. The waves rose higher, the rain fell, and lightning flashed.

It was so rough, the ship almost broke in two.

"God, help us!" cried the sailors. "Please don't let us drown!"

Jonah was below deck, fast asleep. He hadn't even noticed the storm. The captain climbed down to the bottom of the ship to rouse him.

"Wake up!" he shouted. "Help us pray! Perhaps your God will listen to you!

Overboard!

"But God won't listen to me," Jonah told the captain. "This is my fault, because I disobeyed God. I shouldn't be on your ship at all. I'm supposed to be in Nineveh. I guess that's why God sent the storm."

Jonah climbed up on deck with the captain.

"Throw me into the sea!" he yelled to the sailors. "Perhaps then the storm will stop – and you'll be safe."

With a great heave, the sailors tossed Jonah overboard into the sea. The moment he hit the water, the storm stopped.

Was this the end of poor Jonah?

189

A great fish

Story
172

Jonah said,
"In my distress
I called to the
Lord, and he
answered me."

Jonah 2:2 NIV

Although he
had disobeyed
God, Jonah
prayed when
he was in
trouble.

Down, down into the swirling water went Jonah.
He was sure he was going to drown.

Then all of a sudden – *gulp*! Something swallowed
Jonah whole.

He was in the tummy of a huge, great, big,
enormous, giant fish that had been swimming past.
Jonah stayed inside that fish three whole days and
nights.

"Lord, save me!" he prayed from the fish's tummy.

On the beach

God heard Jonah's prayer.

On the third day the huge, great, big, enormous, giant fish spat Jonah out onto the seashore.

Jonah stood up, shook off the seaweed, and wondered what to do next.

Then God spoke to him again.

"Jonah, go to the great city of Nineveh!" God said. "Say to the people there: 'God will punish you, unless you mend your ways.'"

Do you think Jonah obeyed God this time?

"Salvation comes from the Lord."

Jonah 2:9 NIV

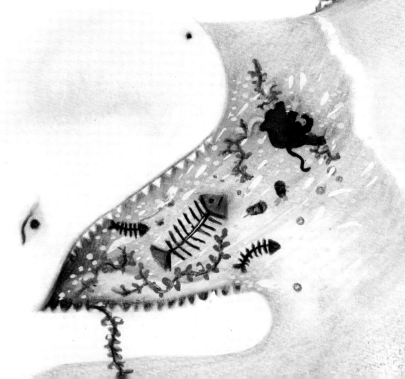

191

Jonah obeys

This time Jonah did just what God told him. He journeyed to Nineveh.

"God is going to destroy your great city," he told its people. "Nineveh will stand for only forty more days!"

The people of Nineveh were terrified.

"We're so sorry!" they prayed. "Forgive us! We want to change."

God heard them.

"I won't destroy your city after all," he told them.

So the ship was saved. Jonah was saved. And the great city of Nineveh was saved too!

The Lord said to Jonah, "Don't you think I should be concerned about that big city?"

Jonah 4:11 CEV

God heard the prayers of the people of Nineveh as well as Jonah's prayers.

Hannah prays

In the Promised Land, on top of a hill, stood God's tent, the tabernacle. There lived the priests, who taught the Israelites to love and obey God.

Every year they held a great festival, and many people came to celebrate.

One year a man brought his wife, Hannah, to the festival. She was sad because they had no children.

"God, please give me a little son," Hannah begged. "When he grows up, I will give him back to you, to help you."

Eli, the high priest, had been listening.

"Go home, Hannah," said the old man gently. "God has listened to you."

"There is no Rock like our God."

1 Samuel 2:2
NIV

What do you ask God for?

A baby for Hannah

As Samuel grew older, the Lord was pleased with him, and so were the people.

1 Samuel 2:26
CEV

Hannah went home feeling much happier. She was sure she would soon have the son she so wanted.

And she did.

"We'll call our little boy Samuel," she said, when the baby arrived. "I'll give him to God to help in the tabernacle, as I promised."

When Samuel had grown old enough, Hannah took him back to God's tent.

Eli, the high priest, was waiting.

"Here is the child I asked God for," Hannah said. "I have brought Samuel to help you in the tabernacle."

Soon Samuel was helping the priests with the jobs they had to do each day.

Did God answer Hannah's prayer?

194

A voice in the night

One night Samuel was asleep in bed.

A voice called, "Samuel, Samuel!"

Samuel woke with a start. He thought it was Eli calling – and ran in to the old man.

"Here I am, Eli!" he said. "You called me."

"I didn't," said Eli. "Go and lie down again."

Samuel went back to bed. But once more he heard the voice call, "Samuel!"

The boy ran to Eli again, saying, "Here I am, Eli – you *did* call me."

The old priest said again, "I didn't call you! Go and lie down again."

Then a third time the voice came: "Samuel, Samuel!"

A third time Samuel went to find Eli.

"Here I am, Eli! I'm *sure* I heard you call," he said.

By now Eli realized it must be God calling Samuel.

"Go and lie down, Samuel," said Eli. "If you hear the voice call again, say, 'Speak, Lord – your helper is listening.'"

"*Speak, for your servant is listening.*"

1 Samuel 3:10
NRSV

Who was calling Samuel?

Samuel listens

Eli said, "He is the Lord, and he will do what's right."

1 Samuel 3:18
CEV

Samuel felt a bit frightened when Eli said this.

But he went back to his room to lie down.

Soon, in the darkness, the voice came again: "Samuel! Samuel!"

This time he answered as Eli had told him: "Speak, Lord – your helper is listening!"

And God spoke to Samuel.

There was sad news. God told Samuel that Eli and his sons had done wrong. Samuel felt worried: he didn't want to tell Eli about this.

In the morning, Eli asked what God had said, so Samuel had to tell him. The old man felt sad.

Why didn't Samuel want to tell Eli what God had said?

The ark is stolen

"The glory has departed from Israel, for the ark of God has been captured."

1 Samuel 4:22
NIV

Was it a good plan to put the ark next to Dagon?

The Israelites were fighting the Philistines again. They kept losing every battle.

Some of the Israelites decided to carry the ark of the covenant into battle with them. They thought it would help them win!

But the Philistines captured the holy ark. They carried it away to one of their cities. There they stood it in a temple, next to the statue of their god, Dagon.

197

A broken god

They said,
"The God of
Israel did this."

1 Samuel 5:7
CEV

The very next morning the Philistines discovered the statue of Dagon lying on its face in front of the ark!

They quickly picked up their image.

The following morning they found Dagon lying in front of the ark again, with his head and hands broken off.

As long as the ark stayed, the Philistines had terrible problems.

"We're being punished by the Israelites' God for stealing the ark," they said. "We *must* get rid of it – or we'll all die!"

What did the Philistines do with the ark?

198

The ark returns

The Philistines decided to send the ark on to the city of Gath. But soon people there started dying. They sent it on to yet another city.

But people saw the ark coming.

"No! We'll die too," they protested. "Send it back to Israel – or all us Philistines will be killed."

So they put the ark on a cart and sent it off toward Israel. When the Israelites saw God's holy ark returning, they were overjoyed.

"No other God is like the Lord!"

1 Samuel 6:20
CEV

God took care of the holy ark – even though his people didn't.

199

Israel demands a king

When young Samuel grew up, he ruled his people,
the Israelites. He taught them how to live in a way
that pleased God.

One day some of the people went to see him.

"You're very old now," they told Samuel.
"We'd like to have a king to reign over us."

"If you get a king, you'll soon start complaining
about him," Samuel told them. "He'll do just as all
kings do – he'll want lots of money."

*Why did
the Israelites
want to have
a king?*

"But we want to be like other
countries," the people said.
"We want a king to rule us."

"All right," Samuel said at
last. "I'll find you a king.
But don't say I haven't
warned you what will
happen!"

Lost donkeys

At this time, there lived a young man named Saul.
His father, Kish, owned great flocks of sheep and herds
of cattle, as well as some wild donkeys.

One day Kish sent for Saul.

"Some of my donkeys have escaped," said Kish.
"Go and see if you can find them."

So Saul set off with a servant in search of the missing
donkeys. But they couldn't find them anywhere.

"Let's go home now," Saul said to his servant.

But they didn't know which way to go!

Then the servant had a bright idea.

"We're close to where old Samuel lives,"
he told Saul. "Let's ask him the
way back."

When Samuel opened
the door to them, his first
thought was, "This young
man looks just like a king!"

Did Saul become king?

*Saul was the
most handsome
man in Israel
– head and
shoulders taller
than anyone
else in the land.*

1 Samuel 9:2
NLT

The best seat

Samuel said,
*"The Lord has
appointed you
to be the leader
of his people
Israel."*

1 Samuel 10:1
NLT

"We're having a big feast," Samuel told Saul. "Please come! And stop worrying about your donkeys – someone has found them already."

Saul went along to Samuel's feast. Another surprise was waiting for him: Samuel put Saul in the top seat!

"Saul would be a really great king," the guests said to one another. "*He'd* soon defeat our enemies."

"The people want a king," Samuel told Saul. "He needs to be young, strong, and fearless. When the time comes, you shall be that king."

*How do you
think Saul felt
after this feast?*

A crown for Saul

Some time later Samuel called for Saul.

"Here's the king God has chosen!"
Samuel announced to the Israelites.
"There's no one like him in the
whole land."

"God save the king!"
shouted the crowds.

In this way, Saul became
the first king of Israel.

The man who went in
search of wild donkeys had
found a royal crown!

*The crowd
shouted, "Long
live the king!"*

1 Samuel 10:24
CEV

*Was Saul a
good king?*

203

"The Lord is my shepherd, I shall not be in want. He makes me lie down in green pastures."

Psalm 23:1–2
NIV

A singing shepherd

Do you remember another boy with lots of older brothers?

In the little town of Bethlehem lived a young shepherd boy named David. He had seven grown-up brothers.

David was a good shepherd. With his sling, he could hurl a stone a long distance. David had killed a hungry lion and an angry bear with his sling.

David also sang beautifully and played the harp.

Samuel's quest

King Saul started well as ruler of Israel – but soon he started to do wrong.

After a time, God said to Samuel, "You must find a new king to rule Israel. Go to Bethlehem and find a man named Jesse. One of his sons shall be the next king."

So Samuel went to Bethlehem. Jesse gave a great feast for him. Samuel inspected Jesse's sons carefully. They were all fine, strong men.

"None of these is the one I've chosen," God told Samuel. "I don't choose people because of the way they look. I see what is in their heart."

"Man looks at the outward appearance, but the Lord looks at the heart."

1 Samuel 16:7
NIV

Who did God choose?

Story
188

David was ruddy, with a fine appearance and handsome features.

1 Samuel 16:12
NIV

God chose the son the others had forgotten about!

A new king

Samuel was puzzled. He turned and asked Jesse, "Are *all* your sons here?"

"All except David, my youngest," replied Jesse. "He's out in the fields, minding my sheep."

"Fetch him in too!" said Samuel.

So one of his brothers went to find David.

As soon as the young shepherd ran in, Samuel knew, "*This* is the one God has chosen. When he's older, this boy will become king of Israel."

Samuel poured oil on David's head, to show everyone that he would be the next king.

206

Scary Goliath

The Philistines were attacking Israel again.

In their army, they had a giant named Goliath. He wasn't afraid of anyone.

"You don't all need to get killed," Goliath shouted at the Israelites. "Just send out a single soldier to fight me. If he wins, the Philistines will be your servants. But if I kill him, you shall serve us! Come on – aren't any of you brave enough to fight me?"

Saul was scared of Goliath, and so were all his soldiers. They stayed in their camp, but day after day Goliath kept yelling at them.

"I challenge Israel's whole army! Choose someone to fight me!"

1 Samuel 17:10
CEV

Who would meet the giant's challenge?

The giant's challenge

"Who does that worthless Philistine think he is? He's making fun of the army of the living God!"

1 Samuel 17:26
CEV

David's brothers all went off to join the army. David was too young and stayed at home.

One day David took some food to his brothers at the army camp. As David was talking to his brothers, Goliath marched out from the Philistine camp.

"Who's brave enough to fight me?" the giant bellowed as usual.

"I will fight Goliath," said young David.

"But you're just a boy!" his brothers laughed.

Why was David so bold?

208

Too big!

David went to find King Saul.

"I'm not afraid of this giant," David told the king.
"I will fight Goliath for you."

"But you're much too young!" said Saul.

"I've killed a lion and a bear!" said David.
"God will help me to beat this bold giant too."

"Go, then!" said Saul.

The king gave David his
helmet and coat of mail.
David put on the heavy
coat and huge helmet,
and strapped on Saul's
mighty sword.

"I can't even walk
in these," said David,
and took them all
off again.

*How was David going
to fight the giant?*

*Saul said
to David,
"Go, and the
Lord be with
you."*

1 Samuel 17:37
NIV

209

Goliath falls

"I come against you in the name of the Lord Almighty."

1 Samuel 17:45
NIV

David trusted God to help him beat the giant.

David went to the brook and chose five smooth pebbles. He tucked them in his little shepherd's pouch.

Then David went out to meet Goliath.
Down the hillside thundered the mighty giant.
When he saw David, he roared with laughter.

"Is he the best you have to fight me?" he bellowed.

David slipped a pebble into his sling, whirled the sling around his head, and let fly.

The stone struck Goliath right on his forehead – and the giant dropped down.

The Philistines watched their hero fall dead.
Then they all ran off.

Story
193

David would play his harp. Saul would relax and feel better.

1 Samuel 16:23
CEV

David escapes

King Saul was often sad and fearful.

"Perhaps some music might make you feel better," said his friends. "We've heard that David plays the harp quite beautifully."

So Saul invited David to play his harp to him when he was feeling sad.

Saul became jealous of David, because people kept saying David was braver than he was.

One day, when David started to play, Saul threw a spear at him.

David saw it coming and dodged out of the way. He fled from the palace.

Did David have any friends who could help?

212

Best friends

David became best friends with Saul's son, Jonathan.

"Why does Saul want to kill me?" he asked Jonathan.

"I'll try to find out," said Jonathan. "If my father is still angry, I'll come and shoot arrows in the field. If I say, 'The arrows are further away,' you'll know you're in danger."

Jonathan discovered that his father, Saul, wanted to kill David. So he went to the field and gave the signal that he had agreed with David.

David ran away.

Jonathan loved David as much as he loved himself.

1 Samuel 20:17
NLT

Do you have a best friend? How can you help your friend?

213

The sleeping king

Saul searched everywhere for David. He wanted desperately to kill him.

Once David and his men found Saul and his soldiers, asleep in a cave.

David crept up and cut off a bit of Saul's robe, without waking him. But he didn't hurt the king.

"It would be wrong for me to harm the man whom God has chosen as king," said David.

Saul said to David, "You are a better man than I am, for you have repaid me good for evil."

1 Samuel 24:17
NLT

Did David harm the man who wanted to kill him?

214

Saul dies

"How the mighty have fallen!"

2 Samuel 1:25
NIV

Although Saul had tried to kill him, David was very sad when the king died.

Not long after, the Philistines defeated Saul's army in a great battle. Many Israelites were killed, including Jonathan. Saul was badly wounded.

"Please kill me," Saul asked his shield-bearer, "so the Philistines can't capture me."

But his shield-bearer wouldn't do it. So Saul killed himself.

The Israelites wept for their king for seven days.

David was very sad when he heard that Saul and Jonathan were both dead.

David is crowned

Story
197

"You... shall be shepherd of my people Israel."

2 Samuel 5:2
NRSV

After Saul died, David became king of Israel, just as Samuel had promised.

People called the Jebusites were living in the city of Jerusalem at that time. David drove them out.

He made Jerusalem the capital city of Israel.

After this time, Jerusalem became a very important city for the Jewish people.

216

Welcoming the ark

David wanted the ark of the covenant to be brought to Jerusalem.

He went to the town where it had been stored for many years and had the ark transported to Jerusalem.

Everyone was very happy. People sang and danced for joy as the ark entered Jerusalem.

At last the ark was back in the chief city of Israel.

David danced before the Lord with all his might.

2 Samuel 6:14
NLT

Why do you think David was so glad that the ark had come to Jerusalem?

217

David keeps a promise

*"I want to
show God's
kindness...
in any way
I can."*

2 Samuel 9:3
CEV

David missed Jonathan very much. He once promised
Jonathan that he would always look after his family.

David sent for an old servant.

"Is anyone in Jonathan's family still alive?" he asked.

"Yes – one of his sons," said the servant. "He's
named Mephibosheth. He was disabled when he was
a young boy."

David sent for Mephibosheth.

"I loved your father, Jonathan – and I want to be
kind to you," David told him. "Please come and live in
my palace with me for the rest of your life."

*David kept
his promise
to his friend,
Jonathan. Do
you try to keep
promises to
your friends?*

A good king

"I will sing and play music for you with all that I am."

Psalm 108:1
CEV

David wrote many songs praising God. You can find some of them in the Bible, in the book of Psalms.

David ruled Israel for forty years. He had many children, and one son, Solomon, became king when David died.

David gave Solomon some helpful advice: "Be a strong king! Trust God and obey his laws."

Did Solomon take his father's advice?

Story 201

God said, "Follow me and obey my commands as your father David did."

1 Kings 3:14
NLT

A wise request

After Solomon became king, God spoke to him one night in a dream.

"What gift would you most like?" God asked him.

"I'm still a young man – and I rule a great nation," replied Solomon. "Please make me wise! I need to make good choices when my people come and ask me what they should do."

God was pleased Solomon hadn't asked for gold.

"I will make you wiser than anyone who has ever been," God promised the king.

What gift would you ask God for?

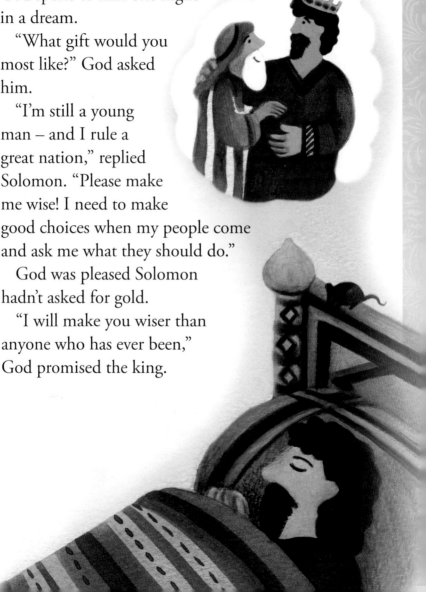

220

Fighting over a baby

One day two women brought a baby to King Solomon's palace.

"It's my baby!" shouted one woman.

"No, it's not – it's mine!" yelled the other.

They were squabbling so noisily that Solomon had to call out, "Please stop! I can't even think!"

Solomon had to judge which of the two women was really the mother of the baby. He pondered long and hard.

Finally the king ordered, "Call in the captain of my guards!"

What did the king do next?

**God gave
Solomon very
great wisdom.**

1 Kings 4:29
NRSV

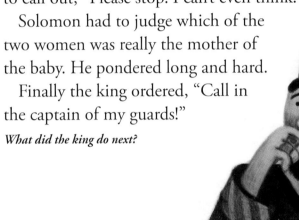

221

Solomon decides

The captain of the guard marched in.

"Take this little baby – and cut it in half!" Solomon commanded. "Each woman can have half!"

"No! No! – please don't do that!" one woman wept. "Please don't hurt the baby! I'd rather *that* woman had the baby than it was cut in two."

At once wise King Solomon knew this woman was the real mother. She loved the baby and wished above all that it lived. She had a true mother's love for it.

Everyone saw how wise God had made Solomon.

Everyone in Israel was amazed when they heard how Solomon had made his decision.

1 Kings 3:28
CEV

Why did Solomon threaten to cut the baby in half?

Solomon builds a temple

King Solomon built a wonderful temple, where his people could worship God. His builders used great stones for the Temple walls. They brought fine wood to cover the walls and construct the furniture.

The ark of the covenant was stored inside, in a windowless room called the Holiest Place. No one was to enter it, except the high priest once a year.

In an outer room stood a golden altar and ten golden lampstands.

King Solomon made the Temple as splendid as possible.

Solomon said, "I am the king of Israel like my father, and I've built a temple for the Lord our God."

1 Kings 8:20
CEV

Where was the ark of the covenant kept before the Temple was built?

223

The Temple is finished

Solomon prayed, "There's not enough room in all of heaven for you, Lord God. How could you possibly live on earth in this Temple I have built?"

1 Kings 8:27
CEV

After seven years, the Temple was completed. King Solomon called his people together to celebrate.

Priests carried the golden ark into the Temple. As the priests came out again, the glory of God appeared. It filled the Temple like a huge cloud.

"O God of Israel, hear the prayers of your people," Solomon asked. "Listen to us, and help us always."

Afterward, the Israelites enjoyed a great feast that lasted a whole week!

Do you remember what was inside the ark of the covenant?

A queen's visit

The riches of King Solomon were famous all over the world. He ate off gold dishes, and his throne was made of ivory. He owned hundreds of chariots and thousands of horses.

Everyone knew how wise he was too. People came to Solomon from all over the world to ask his advice.

The queen of Sheba once visited Solomon. She asked him many difficult questions – and he answered them all!

The queen of Sheba said, "The Lord has always loved Israel, so he has given them a king who will rule fairly and honestly."

1 Kings 10:9
CEV

Did God answer Solomon's prayer to make him wise?

225

The worst king

After Solomon died, his kingdom split into two – the kingdom of Israel and the kingdom of Judah. Both kingdoms were ruled sometimes by good kings and sometimes by bad kings.

Ahab was the worst king of all! He married Jezebel, who prayed to the false god Baal. Ahab started to worship Baal too. He even built a temple for Baal.

God sent Elijah to King Ahab. Elijah was one of God's special messengers, or "prophets".

He told the people what God specially wanted to say to them.

"Ahab," said Elijah, "you have done so many bad things that God says there will be no rain in your kingdom for many years!"

Ahab felt very angry. He wanted to harm Elijah.

Did God protect Elijah?

Elijah runs away

Elijah ran away from Ahab to the desert. He lived there alone, beside a tiny stream.

Elijah couldn't find anything to eat in the desert, so he prayed, "Lord God, please give me some food."

God sent big, black birds called ravens to Elijah. They carried food to him in their beaks.

There was so little rain that one day the tiny stream completely dried up.

Now Elijah had nothing to drink. What was he to do?

"Go to the village of Zarephath," God told him. "I have told a widow there to take care of you."

The Lord said, "Eat the food I've told the ravens to bring you."

1 Kings 17:4
CEV

Elijah received food from the sky!

227

Story 209

Elijah asks for food

"The Lord God of Israel has promised that your jar of flour won't run out."

1 Kings 17:14
CEV

God was still looking after his prophet, Elijah.

As Elijah arrived in Zarephath, he saw a woman picking up sticks.

"May I have a drink of water and some bread?" he asked.

The woman shook her head.

"I have no bread – just a handful of flour and a drop of oil," she said. "I'm going to light a fire and bake a last loaf for my son and myself. Then we will starve."

"Bake the loaf, and give me some bread!" said Elijah. "God has promised that your flour and oil will not run out until it rains and we have crops again."

So the widow baked a loaf and gave Elijah some bread.

From that day on, until the rain came, she always had enough food for herself, her son, and for the prophet Elijah.

228

Alive again!

*The woman
told Elijah,
"Now I know
for sure that
you are a man
of God, and
that the Lord
truly speaks
through you."*

1 Kings 17:24
NLT

One day this woman's son fell sick and died. She was heartbroken.

"This woman has helped me, Lord," Elijah said to God. "Why have you let her little boy die?"

Elijah prayed to God three times, "Please give back this child's life!"

And the boy came back to life!

Elijah took him to his mother.

"Look!" he said. "Your son is alive again!"

*Can you think
of any other
people in the
Bible who were
brought back
to life?*

229

Troublemaker!

When Ahab saw Elijah, he said to him, "Is that you, you troubler of Israel?"

1 Kings 18:17
NIV

Three years went by with no rain.

"Go and see King Ahab again," God said to Elijah at last. So the prophet left the woman's house and went back to Ahab's palace.

"It's you, Elijah," said the king, "– the great troublemaker! I'm amazed you dare to come here! You've brought nothing but suffering to my kingdom."

"Nonsense!" said Elijah. "It's you, Ahab, who has brought these troubles to your kingdom. God has punished you and your people. It's your fault alone there has been no rain."

Who won the contest?

The king frowned. But he knew Elijah was right.

"Now let's have a competition!" Elijah went on. "We'll find out whose god is for real – your god, Baal, or my God." Ahab agreed.

230

A contest

"Call all your people to Mount Carmel," Elijah said to Ahab. "Bring the prophets of Baal too."

They all gathered at Mount Carmel to set up the contest. King Ahab's prophets ran around, collecting stones to build an altar for their god, Baal.

Elijah selected stones to build an altar for his God. Then the competition began.

"How long will you waver between two opinions? If the Lord is God, follow him."

1 Kings 18:21
NIV

There were many prophets of Baal. Did they win?

231

Story
213

There was no response, no one answered, no one paid attention.

1 Kings 18:29
NIV

No answer!

First Ahab's prophets laid offerings on their altar. Then they prayed – and waited for Baal to send fire to burn up their sacrifice.

Nothing happened!

The king's prophets screamed to Baal to send fire. No fire came.

"Pray louder!" Elijah mocked them. "Perhaps your god is asleep. Or perhaps he's out hunting and can't hear you!"

They shouted louder and louder. But nothing happened. Finally they gave up.

What did Elijah do next?

232

Fire from heaven

By this time it was evening.

God's prophet, Elijah, placed an offering on his altar. Then he poured water over the offering, to make it more difficult to catch fire.

"God in heaven," he prayed, "send fire on my altar!"

Fire came.

It burned up the offering, the stones, and even the water.

Now the people of Israel saw that Elijah's God was the true God – not King Ahab's god, Baal.

"The Lord – he is God! The Lord – he is God!"

1 Kings 18:39
NIV

Do you think King Ahab was pleased about what happened?

233

Story 215

A tiny cloud

"Look, a little cloud no bigger than a person's hand is rising out of the sea."

1 Kings 18:44
NRSV

"Look out to sea!"
Elijah told his servant.
"Tell me what you see."
The servant came back.
"I can't see anything."
Elijah said, "Look again!"
This happened seven
times. The seventh time
the servant reported,
"I can see a tiny cloud
on the horizon.
It's no bigger than
a hand."

Why did Elijah tell his servant to look out to sea?

God sends rain

"Good!" said Elijah. "Now go and tell Ahab
he'd better get down the mountain. Soon it will
be raining so hard, he won't be able drive his chariot."
  As he spoke, the little cloud grew larger.
  Soon the sky was black with storm clouds.
  The wind blew fiercely, and finally rain came.
It poured! King Ahab raced home in his chariot.
  Elijah ran even faster and reached the city first!

*The Lord gave
special strength
to Elijah. He
tucked his
cloak into his
belt and ran
ahead of Ahab's
chariot.*

1 Kings 18:46
NLT

God kept his
word: now it
started to rain
again.

235

Fed by an angel

The Lord asked, "Elijah, why are you here?"

1 Kings 19:9
CEV

But King Ahab and his horrible wife, Jezebel, still wanted to kill Elijah. He had to run away again to the desert. When he arrived there, he felt so tired and miserable he lay down and fell asleep.

Someone tapped Elijah on his shoulder.

He jumped up, startled.

Had Ahab's soldiers caught him?

No – it was an angel! God's angel had come to make Elijah dinner.

After a good meal, Elijah felt strong enough to set off again on his long journey.

God looked after his prophet when he was in danger.

A helper for Elijah

Elijah heard a gentle voice speaking.

"Go and find a man named Elisha," it said. "He will help you – and he'll take on your job after you go."

God was telling Elijah he was no longer on his own.

Elijah left the desert straight away. Soon he found Elisha, working in a field.

Elijah placed his cloak around the young man's shoulders, to show he wanted Elisha to become his helper.

Elijah was getting old. Now his young helper, Elisha, went with him everywhere.

Elisha then left his oxen and ran after Elijah. "Let me kiss my father and mother goodbye," he said, "and then I will come with you."

1 Kings 19:20
NIV

Do you think Elijah was pleased to have a younger helper?

Ahab steals a vineyard

*Elijah said,
"Ahab, you have
managed to
do everything
the Lord hates.
Now you will
be punished."*

1 Kings 21:20
CEV

A man named Naboth had a vineyard near King Ahab's palace. The king saw it – and wanted to have it.

"This vineyard has belonged to my family for years," said Naboth. "I'm not selling it." Ahab went to bed in a sulk.

"What's the matter with you?" asked Jezebel.

Ahab told her.

"But you're the king: you can have anything you want," said Jezebel.

So Jezebel had Naboth killed.

"Now Naboth's vineyard is yours," she told Ahab.

But Elijah came to see Ahab again. "You've stolen Naboth's vineyard and had him killed," said Elijah. "Now you too will die."

*Do you
think it was
easy for Elijah
to tell King
Ahab that
God would
punish him?*

238

Chariot of fire

One day Elijah and Elisha were walking along together when, all of a sudden, a chariot and horses of fire appeared. The fiery horses drove between the two men.

Whoosh! The chariot of fire carried Elijah up to heaven. Elisha watched, amazed, as Elijah disappeared.

As Elijah flew upward, his coat flew off. It landed on the ground. Elisha picked up Elijah's coat thoughtfully. Now it was his!

Elisha went sadly on his way.

Elijah went up to heaven in a whirlwind.

2 Kings 2:11
NIV

It must have been a bit scary to see a fiery chariot appear.

239

*Elisha said,
"The Lord has
made this water
pure again."*

2 Kings 2:21
CEV

Elisha the
prophet did
many miracles.

Good water

Some men came to see Elisha the prophet.

"We're from the city of Jericho," they told him. "The water there makes us sick if we drink it. And it poisons the crops."

"Bring me a bowl of salt!" said Elisha.

They gave him salt, and he threw it into the spring.

"Now the land will produce plenty of good crops again," he said.

And it did!

Lots of oil

Elisha met a woman as he was walking through a village one day.

"I owe a man a great deal of money!" she told him. "And all I have is one tiny pot of olive oil."

"Borrow as many empty jars as you can," Elisha told her. "Take them home and pour your oil into them."

The woman went all around her village, borrowing from friends. Soon she'd collected up lots of jars, pots, jugs, pitchers, bowls, and bottles. She took them all home.

The woman started to pour oil from her pot. She poured, and poured, and poured. The oil just kept coming! Soon she'd filled every single jar in the house.

The woman took her jars, pots, jugs, pitchers, bowls, and bottles to market and sold the oil. Soon she had enough money to pay back everything she owed. And she still had enough left to buy food for her own family.

"I have nothing but a small bottle of olive oil."

2 Kings 4:2
CEV

Elisha had done another miracle, with God's help.

A room for Elisha

*"I know that
this man who
often comes our
way is a holy
man of God."*

2 Kings 4:9
NIV

God gave this
kind woman
a son after she
helped Elisha.

Elisha often stopped for dinner at the home
of a rich woman.

"This prophet is a real man of God,"
she told her husband. "Let's build a little room
for him to stay in, on the roof of our house."

"You've done so many kind things for me,"
Elisha said to the woman one day. "I'd like to do
something for you in return."

"Thank you," she replied.
"But we really don't need anything."

"Can you think what we could do for her?" Elisha
asked his servant, Gehazi.

"This woman has no children,"
Gehazi told him.

So Elisha told her, "I promise
by this time next year you will
have a son."

She could hardly believe
it. But the next year she
had a baby boy.

242

The general's disease

Naaman was an important general in the army.
But he had a horrible skin disease, called leprosy.

Naaman's wife had a young Israelite servant girl.

"I do wish my master could meet the prophet
Elisha," said the girl. "I'm sure Elisha's God
could help him."

Naaman heard about this.

"Who is this man, Elisha?" he asked the girl.
"And how can I find him?"

Soon Naaman set off to meet Elisha.

Do you think Elisha helped the general?

*"If only my
master would
see the prophet
who is in
Samaria! He
would cure him
of his leprosy!"*

2 Kings 5:3
NIV

Elisha's cure

Elisha lived in a simple cottage. He was very surprised to find the proud general at his door.

"I have a horrid skin disease," explained Naaman. "My servant girl said you might be able to help me."

"Go and wash in the River Jordan seven times," Elisha instructed him. "After that, you'll be completely well again."

Naaman wasn't sure about this. It sounded rather silly. The Jordan was a dirty, muddy river. How would washing in mucky water help him?

"Master – just do as the prophet says!" urged Naaman's servants.

Naaman asked, "Are not Abana and Pharpar, the rivers of Damascus, better than any of the waters of Israel?"

2 Kings 5:12
NIV

It was a strange thing to ask: did the general do it?

244

Clean skin

Naaman decided to do as Elisha had told him.
He went to the River Jordan to wash.

Naaman dipped himself in the river – once, twice,
three times… After the seventh time, the leprosy
vanished! Naaman's skin was as smooth and clear as a
baby's. Elisha's God had healed him.

Naaman went to thank Elisha.

"Please accept these gifts of gold and silver," he said.

"No. I never take payment," said Elisha.

"God doesn't want me to."

Naaman said,
"Now I know
that there is no
God in all the
world except in
Israel."

2 Kings 5:15
NRSV

**Why do you
think God
didn't want
Elisha to be
paid to heal
people?**

245

Hezekiah cleans up

Hezekiah prayed, "O Lord, God of Israel... you alone are God over all the kingdoms of the earth."

2 Kings 19:15
NIV

When Hezekiah became king, the Temple in Jerusalem hadn't been used for many years. Hezekiah wanted to open it up again.

"Please clean out God's house," he told the priests.

"Everything is tidy and ready to use," they told the king sixteen days later.

The very next day Hezekiah went to the Temple to worship God. How happy the people were to pray in the great Temple once again!

Why do you think the Temple hadn't been used?

246

Passover again

God heard them, for their prayer reached heaven.

2 Chronicles 30:27 NIV

God's people hadn't celebrated the Passover festival for many years. Now King Hezekiah wanted to hold the Passover feast again. He invited his people to come to Jerusalem to celebrate the festival with him.

Usually Passover was held in April. But there was so much to get ready that the king decided to hold it in May instead.

Passover lasted for seven days, filled with singing, music, and reading the books of Moses.

People were enjoying themselves so much that they stayed for another whole week!

Do you remember why the Jews celebrated Passover?

Josiah followed
the example
of his ancestor
David and
always obeyed
the Lord.

2 Chronicles 34:2
CEV

*If you became
king, what
would you do?*

A boy king

Josiah was only eight years old when he became king.
But he loved God and wanted to please him.

The people of Israel had not been looking after the
Temple. Bits of it were falling down. So Josiah told
his workmen to start mending God's Temple. Priests
played music and sang, while the men repaired the
Temple.

Everyone wanted God's house to become a beautiful
place of worship again.

Josiah's discovery

The high priest was also working in the Temple. Suddenly, he discovered an old scroll. He saw it was a copy of the laws that God had given to Moses.

"Look, here is the Law of Moses," the high priest said to King Josiah. "Let me read some of it to you."

Josiah listened carefully. He'd never heard it before. Now he realized that his people hadn't been keeping God's rules.

He felt very bad about this.

"No wonder we've had so many troubles," Josiah said to the high priest. "Please pray for our country."

And Josiah made sure his people followed God's way the rest of his reign.

The people did not turn away from the Lord God of their ancestors for the rest of Josiah's reign as king.

2 Chronicles 34:33 CEV

How did Josiah find out about God's rules for his people?

249

The Temple burns

They burned
the house of
God and broke
down the wall
of Jerusalem.

*2 Chronicles
36:19 NRSV*

Terrible times now came for the people of God, the Jews. The mighty Babylonians attacked Jerusalem. They surrounded the city: no one could bring in food for its people. King Zedekiah tried to escape, but the Babylonians captured him.

After many months, the army of Babylon destroyed Jerusalem and burned the beautiful Temple. They smashed the city walls and killed many of the people. The rest they carried off to become slaves in Babylon.

*Do you think the
Jews ever returned
to Jerusalem?*

Daniel's diet

After Jerusalem was destroyed, a young man named Daniel was one of the prisoners taken to Babylon. There the great King Nebuchadnezzar chose Daniel and his three best friends – Shadrach, Meshach, and Abednego – to go to a special school.

The boys were given food and wine used in the worship of Babylon's gods.

"Please excuse us from eating this food," they said.

"If it makes you weak and sick, the king will punish me," said their teacher.

"Give us just vegetables and water for ten days," said Daniel. "We'll be fine. You'll see!"

Soon Daniel and his friends had become the best students.

God made the four young men smart and wise.

Daniel 1:17
CEV

Why didn't Daniel and his friends want to eat the food they were given?

251

"We won't bow!"

"The God we serve... will rescue us from your hand, O King."

Daniel 3:17 NIV

These three brave men were in danger! Did God protect them?

King Nebuchadnezzar decided to build a huge statue.

"When the band plays," he declared, "everyone must bow to the statue. Those who don't will be thrown into a blazing hot fire."

The band played – and everyone bowed to the king's statue.

But Shadrach, Meshach, and Abednego refused to bow.

"Respect me!" yelled the king. "Unless you want to be thrown into the flames!"

"O King, even if you put us in the fire, God will protect us," said the young men. "We will never worship anyone but God. We will *not* bow to your statue!"

How many men?

"Make the fire seven times hotter!" shouted the angry king. "Then throw these three men in the flames!"

The soldiers obeyed. They slung the three men in. Nebuchadnezzar watched in amazement.

"We put three men in the fire," he said. "Now I see four men in the flames! And they don't seem to be hurt."

"Shadrach! Meshach! Abednego!" called the king. "Come out of the fire!"

The three men stepped out unharmed. Their hair wasn't even singed.

Nebuchadnezzar was astonished.

"Let us worship the God of Shadrach, Meshach, and Abednego!" he said.

Nebuchadnezzar said, "Praise be to the God of Shadrach, Meshach, and Abednego!"

Daniel 3:28 NIV

Even in the fire, God was with them.

The mystery hand

Years later Nebuchadnezzar's son, Belshazzar, became king of Babylon. One night he held a great party.

"Bring out the gold cups we took from the Temple in Jerusalem," he ordered.

Then Belshazzar drank wine from the holy cups!

All of a sudden, he saw a mysterious hand writing in a foreign language on the wall of his palace. Belshazzar was very scared!

"Send for Daniel!" said the queen. "His God will be able to explain the writing."

Daniel came quickly.

"God says you are unfit to rule," said Daniel. "Enemies will capture your kingdom."

That very night the Persian army captured Babylon. Belshazzar was killed.

How would you feel if you saw a mysterious hand writing on the wall?

A faultless man

Darius the Great now became king. He chose Daniel as one of his top advisors.

The king's other advisors grew jealous of Daniel. Why did the king always listen to him? They tried hard to find some fault in Daniel – but Daniel never did anything wrong. The king could always trust him.

Every morning, every lunchtime, and every night Daniel prayed to the living God.

What did the jealous advisors do?

Daniel did his work so much better than the other governors and officials.

Daniel 6:3 CEV

255

A trap for Daniel

Three times
a day Daniel
got down on
his knees and
prayed, giving
thanks to his
God.

Daniel 6:10
NIV

The jealous advisors hatched a plot against Daniel.

"O King Darius!" they said. "You only are wise and powerful. Make a new law saying that no one must pray to anyone except you! If anyone disobeys, he will be thrown into a pit of lions."

"Write out this new law for me," Darius told his advisors.

Then trumpeters announced this new law throughout his kingdom: "No one must pray to anyone except King Darius!"

Did Daniel stop praying?

Sneaks!

*"No written
law of the
Medes and
Persians can be
changed."*

Daniel 6:15
CEV

The king had
made a foolish
law. Now he
had to go by it.

Now the jealous advisors hid outside Daniel's house.
They saw him kneel and pray to God – just as he did
every day.

They rushed back to King Darius.

"Daniel is still praying to his God," they hissed.

"Oh dear!" said Darius the Great. He was really
sorry, because he respected Daniel a lot.

"Daniel must be thrown into the lions' pit,"
demanded the advisors.

The foolish king had to agree.

Story
239

"The God of Daniel... is the living God."

Daniel 6:26
NIV

God saved Daniel from certain death.

Into the pit

Darius's soldiers threw Daniel into the pit of lions.

The king didn't sleep that night. He couldn't stop thinking of poor Daniel and the lions.

When morning came, Darius hurried to the pit.

"Daniel!" he shouted. "Are you all right?"

To his astonishment, Daniel replied, "I'm fine. Not a scratch!"

Then he explained, "God sent an angel to shut the lions' mouths."

"Get Daniel out – now!" shouted Darius.

When Daniel had been released from the pit, Darius ordered, "Go, arrest those wicked advisors who trapped Daniel!

"From today, everyone must respect Daniel's God," said Darius. "He is the living God. He saved Daniel from the lions. This is the law of the Medes and Persians. It *cannot* be changed!"

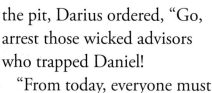

259

Story 240

Esther saves her people

For the Jews it was a time of happiness and joy.

Esther 8:16
NIV

Esther was a beautiful Jewish girl. She was married to Xerxes, the great king of Persia.

One day Esther heard a man named Haman making a plot.

"I'm going to kill all Queen Esther's people, the Jews," said Haman.

Esther was very worried, so she made a plan.

At dinner, Esther told her husband, the king, "Haman is plotting to get rid of my people."

The king was very angry. He sent soldiers to arrest Haman.

Esther had saved her people, the Jews.

Esther was in a foreign land. But she bravely helped her people.

260

Returning home

It was seventy years since God's people had been taken from Jerusalem. Cyrus the Great now ruled Babylon.

"Anyone who wants to return to Jerusalem is free to do so," he announced.

Nearly fifty thousand people now returned to Jerusalem. Cyrus sent back with them the gold and silver Nebuchadnezzar had stolen from the Temple.

When the people arrived back in Jerusalem, they began to rebuild the Temple.

But old men shook their heads sadly. "It will never be as beautiful as the Temple that Solomon built!" they said.

All the people gave a great shout of praise to the Lord, because the foundation of the house of the Lord was laid.

Ezra 3:11
NIV

Why did the Jews want to rebuild the Temple?

261

Rebuilding Jerusalem

A Jewish man named Nehemiah was cup-bearer to King Cyrus.

Nehemiah asked some friends who had been back to Jerusalem, "Are the city walls being rebuilt?"

"The work is slow, and the walls are still in ruins," they told him.

The king noticed that Nehemiah looked very sad.

"What is the matter?" asked the king.

"Your Majesty, I'm sad because my beautiful city is still in ruins. Can I go back and make sure the repair work gets done?"

"Yes, you may," said the king.

"Why should my face not look sad when the city where my fathers are buried lies in ruins?"

Nehemiah 2:3
NIV

Although he was king of another country, Cyrus wanted to help Nehemiah rebuild Jerusalem.

Weak walls

Story
243

So Nehemiah journeyed across the desert to Jerusalem.

He discovered that enemies were preventing the Jews from rebuilding their city.

"First of all we need to build up the walls," Nehemiah told the workers. "That way, we can keep our enemies out. Then we can do the rest of the building work. Now let's get on with it!"

The people got busy.

But their enemies just mocked them.

"Those walls are so weak, a fox could crumble them!" they jeered.

Did Nehemiah finish the work?

"If even a fox climbed up on it, he would break down their wall of stones!"

Nehemiah 4:3

NIV

Workers with weapons

The Jewish people kept working. Now enemies started to attack them.

"Carry your weapons at all times," Nehemiah ordered his men.

Half the Jews stood guard while the others built up the walls. Everyone carried a sword.

Fifty-two days after they started work, they completed the walls of Jerusalem!

It must have been difficult building a wall when enemies might attack at any moment.

Celebration!

The Jewish people were no longer prisoners.
Many had returned to their own land.

They had finished rebuilding the walls of Jerusalem.
They had completed the new Temple.

They had brought back the gold and silver bowls
and other treasures stolen from the old Temple.

Now they celebrated.

They marched to the gleaming Temple and gave
thanks to God.

*"Blessed be
your glorious
name...
You alone are
the Lord."*

Nehemiah 9:5–6
NIV

How glad
God's people
were to return
to their own
land!

NEW TESTAMENT

Speechless

Zechariah was a priest in the Temple. He and his wife, Elizabeth, were now quite old – and they had no children.

It was Zechariah's turn to help in the Temple. Suddenly, an angel named Gabriel stood beside him.

"Don't be afraid, Zechariah!" said the angel. "I have good news. You and Elizabeth are going to have a baby boy! You must name him John. He will bring the people back to God."

Zechariah was amazed. "How can this happen?" he asked. "My wife is too old to have a baby."

"Because you don't believe what God has promised," said Gabriel, "you won't be able to speak until the baby is born!"

Why didn't Zechariah believe the angel's message?

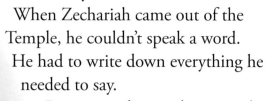

When Zechariah came out of the Temple, he couldn't speak a word. He had to write down everything he needed to say.

But just as the angel promised, Elizabeth soon found she was expecting a baby.

Mary's visitor

Elizabeth's cousin, a young woman named Mary,
lived in the little town of Nazareth.

One day the angel Gabriel visited her too.

Mary was amazed – and a bit frightened.

"Mary!" said the angel.
"There's no need to be worried.
I have wonderful news from your
Heavenly Father! You are going to
have a baby. You must name him
Jesus. God is sending him to
save the world."

Mary was puzzled.

"How can this happen?"
she asked. "I'm not even
married yet."

"God will make this
happen," said Gabriel.
"With God, nothing is
impossible."

"I will do whatever
God wants!" said Mary.

*Mary said,
"With all my
heart I praise
the Lord."*

Luke 1:46 CEV

*How do you
think Mary felt
when the angel
appeared?*

269

*Zechariah said,
"Praise the
Lord, the God
of Israel!
He has come to
save his people."*

Luke 1:68 CEV

We will find
out later how
John prepared
the way for
Jesus.

A baby's name

Mary decided to visit her cousin Elizabeth.

"You are really blessed," Elizabeth told her,
"because God has chosen you."

A few months later Elizabeth's baby arrived.

"Name him Zechariah, like his father," said friends.

"No!" said Elizabeth. "He will be named *John*."

Then they asked Zechariah. He wrote, "His name
is John."

At that very moment, Zechariah was able to
speak again!

"God is sending us someone who will save
the world," said Zechariah. "My son will
prepare the way
for him."

Joseph dreams

Mary loved a kind and good man named Joseph, the village carpenter. They were engaged to be married.

Soon after Gabriel visited Mary, Joseph had a dream. In his dream, an angel told him, "Joseph, you must look after Mary. When her baby arrives, you must name him 'Jesus'."

So Mary and Joseph got married straight away.

Near the time for Mary's baby to be born, soldiers nailed up a notice in Nazareth.

It said, "Everyone must go back to the town where they were born, to register their name."

The angel said, "Mary will give birth to a son, and you are to give him the name Jesus, because he will save his people from their sins."

Matthew 1:21
NIV

Do you know the name of Joseph's home town?

271

A long journey

Joseph and Mary had to travel to Joseph's home town, Bethlehem, many miles away.

They set out on the long journey.

Mary rode a little donkey, and Joseph walked alongside. Mary felt very tired.

At last they arrived in Bethlehem. It was very busy.

Lots of other people had come to the town to register their names too.

"How will we find anywhere to stay?" asked Mary.

"We'll try to find a room in an inn," said Joseph.

Because Joseph was a descendant of King David, he had to go to Bethlehem in Judea, David's ancient home.

Luke 2:4 NLT

Where did they stay that night?

No room!

Joseph found an inn and knocked on the door.

"Can you let us have a room?" he asked.

"No, I'm sorry," said the innkeeper. "We're full. There's not a bed to be had in the whole town!"

Then the innkeeper saw Mary's disappointed face.

"I do have a little stable where the animals sleep," he added. "You can sleep there. It's the best I can offer, I'm afraid."

The tired visitors decided to spend the night there, in the simple stable.

And while they were there, the time came for her baby to be born.

Luke 2:6 NLT

It seemed a strange place for this special baby to be born.

273

Mary wrapped him in cloths and placed him in a manger, because there was no room for them in the inn.

Luke 2:7 NIV

The Son of God was born in a borrowed stable.

A baby is born

There in the stable, among the donkeys and cows, Mary's precious baby was born.

Mary looked at him lovingly.

She wrapped her baby around and around, in a long piece of soft cloth, to keep him warm.

"Joseph, we don't have a cradle for our baby," said Mary.

Joseph put clean straw in the animals' feed box.

"I've made a little bed for baby Jesus," he said.

Joseph laid the baby gently in the manger.

Soon Jesus was fast asleep on the straw.

275

The angel's message

It was dark in the fields outside Bethlehem. But the shepherds were still awake, making sure their sheep were safe.

Suddenly, a piercing, bright light shone down. The shepherds felt scared.

"There's no need to be afraid!" said the angel.

"I have good news that will bring joy to all people!"

The shepherds listened in wonder.

Who were the first people to hear that Jesus was born?

The shepherds' search

"Tonight your king has been born in Bethlehem," the angel told them. "You will find him lying in a manger. Go – see for yourselves!"

Suddenly, a whole crowd of angels filled the sky, singing, "Glory to God on high, and peace to his people on earth!"

The light faded, and the night was quiet again.

"Goodness! We've seen angels!" said one shepherd.

"A king has been born. Tonight – here in Bethlehem!"

"Let's see if we can find him!"

They rushed off into Bethlehem to search for the baby king, leaving their sheep on the hillside.

"You will find him dressed in baby clothes and lying on a bed of hay."

Luke 2:12 CEV

Do you think the shepherds were scared or excited by the angel's message?

As the shepherds returned to their sheep, they were praising God and saying wonderful things about him.

Luke 2:20 CEV

At the stable

The shepherds soon found the little stable.

They peered inside and saw Mary, Joseph, and baby Jesus lying in a manger.

They all crowded in to look at the baby. Then the shepherds knelt down.

They told Mary and Joseph excitedly what the angel had told them.

Then, noticing Mary was very tired, the shepherds crept out and went back to look after their sheep.

Mary kept thinking about everything they had said.

What do you think the shepherds told their friends about this night?

A happy old man

Mary and Joseph went to Jerusalem, to take baby Jesus
to God's Temple.

There they met an old man named Simeon.

God had promised Simeon, "You won't die until you
see the baby who will save the world."

As soon as Simeon saw baby Jesus, he knew this was
the one that God had promised.

He cradled little Jesus in his arms.

"Now I can die in peace, Lord,"
he said. "You have kept your promise
to me."

An old lady named Anna
was also in the Temple. She
too knew that Jesus was the
expected one. She hurried
off to tell everyone she met,
"The promised one has
been born!"

*Simeon said,
"With my own
eyes I have seen
what you have
done to save
your people."*

Luke 2:30 CEV

Anna and
Simeon had
been waiting
to see the baby
who would
save the world.

A new star

Wise men from
the East came
to Jerusalem,
asking, "Where
is the child...
born king of
the Jews?"

Matthew 2:1–2
NRSV

**What did
Herod know
about the
new king?**

Far away in the East lived some very
wise men who studied the stars.

Late one night one of them
exclaimed, "I've never seen
that star before!"

"It's a special sign," said
another. "It means a new
king has been born."

"Then we must follow this star
and find him," they all agreed.

So the wise men set out on a long journey,
following the special, new star.

Crossing deserts and wastelands, hills and valleys,
the wise men came at last to Jerusalem,
to the palace of King Herod.

A new king

"Where can we find the newborn king?"
the wise men asked Herod. "We've seen his star
in the East and have come to worship him."

When King Herod heard this, he got very upset.

"I'm the king," he thought. "I don't want another
king taking my crown away!"

So Herod called for his advisors.

"Do you know anything about a new king?"
he asked them. "And if so – where will he be born?"

The advisors scuttled off.

"Our holy books say that a new
king will be born in Bethlehem,"
they told him, when
they returned.

*"A ruler will
come from
Bethlehem
who will be
the shepherd
for my people
Israel."*

Matthew 2:6
NLT

**Was King
Herod happy
to hear that
Jesus had
been born?**

Herod's lie

Story 259

When King Herod heard about this, he was worried, and so was everyone else in Jerusalem.

Matthew 2:3
CEV

King Herod called in the wise men again.

"Go – search for this child!" Herod told them. "When you've found him, come and tell me where he is. I would *love* to go and worship him too."

But Herod was lying.

He really wanted to harm the baby when he found him. He didn't want anyone else claiming to be king!

Did Herod harm baby Jesus?

282

Rich gifts

The star led the wise men once again. It went ahead of them, until it stopped over the house in Bethlehem where Jesus was.

Inside, they found young Jesus with his mother, Mary. When the wise men saw Jesus, they knelt before him.

They had brought with them costly presents: gold and precious scents, called frankincense and myrrh. They set down their gifts for the little boy.

When the wise men saw the star, they were filled with joy!

Matthew 2:10
NLT

The wise men brought Jesus gifts fit for a king.

Story 261

They went back home by another road.

Matthew 2:12
CEV

God protected baby Jesus.

A different route

That same night God warned the wise men in a dream.

"Don't go back to King Herod!" an angel told them. "He wants to harm the baby."

So the wise men journeyed home a different way.

Escape to Egypt!

After the wise men had left, Joseph had a dream too.

"Get up immediately!" an angel told him. "Take Jesus and his mother, and flee to Egypt. Herod is searching for the boy. He wants to harm Jesus."

Then the angel added, "Stay in Egypt, until I tell you it's safe to return home to Nazareth."

Joseph woke Mary, and they set off for Egypt, carrying little Jesus.

When Herod found out that the wise men from the East had tricked him, he was very angry.

Matthew 2:16
CEV

Joseph obeyed God and took Jesus and Mary to a safe place.

285

*The child
Jesus grew. He
became strong
and wise, and
God blessed
him.*

Luke 2:40 CEV

Jesus learned
to read the
books of the
Law that
Moses had
written.

Jesus grows up

After King Herod died, Joseph had another dream.
"Now it's safe to go home," God told him.

They set off on the long journey back to Nazareth,
where Mary and Joseph had lived before Jesus was born.

Jesus grew up with Mary and Joseph in Nazareth.
Joseph worked as a carpenter, and Jesus helped him in
his workshop, sawing and hammering.

When he was old enough, Jesus started to go
to school. He listened carefully to the lessons and
remembered everything he was taught. How proud his
mother Mary was!

Jesus visits Jerusalem

Once a year the Jewish people celebrated the great
Passover festival. They loved to go to Jerusalem,
where the great Temple stood.

When Jesus was twelve years old, Mary said,
"This year you can come with us. You've learned the
Law of God. It's time you came to the Temple."

It was an exciting journey, over the hills to Jerusalem.

As they neared the city, they could see the Temple,
gleaming white and gold in the sun.

*Every year
Jesus' parents
went to
Jerusalem for
the festival of
Passover.*

Luke 2:41 NRSV

**Look at page
129 to remind
yourself about
the Passover
meal.**

287

In God's house

Story
265

The boy Jesus stayed behind in Jerusalem, but they were unaware of it.

Luke 2:43 NIV

Where might Mary and Joseph have looked for Jesus?

When they arrived, Mary, Joseph, and Jesus went to the Temple to pray and worship.

"This is the house of God, my Heavenly Father," thought Jesus.

In the Temple, he met wise men and priests.

Too soon they had to start the long walk back to Nazareth. Mary didn't see Jesus all day.

Nobody seemed to have seen Jesus since they had left Jerusalem.

Mary and Joseph felt quite worried.

"We need to go back," said Joseph.

So back they went to Jerusalem. But they still couldn't find Jesus.

Mary finds Jesus

"There's only one place left to look for Jesus," said Mary at last, "– the Temple."

There, as Mary guessed, they found Jesus.

All who heard Jesus were amazed at his understanding and his answers.

Luke 2:47 NRSV

What did Jesus' answer to Mary mean?

Jesus had found the priests and wise men again. He had been asking them questions.

The old men were amazed that this boy knew so much about the Law of God.

"We've been looking everywhere for you," said Mary. "We were *very* worried."

"I had to come to my Father's house, to learn the things I need to know," said Jesus.

This time Jesus did set off for home with Mary and Joseph.

Story
267

Isaiah the prophet wrote about John when he said, "In the desert someone is shouting, 'Get the road ready for the Lord!'"

Luke 3:4 CEV

When John was born, an angel told his parents he would bring his people back to God.

Cousin John

Jesus' cousin, John, was different from other men. He lived in the desert. He wore clothes made of rough camel's hair. He ate food that he found in the desert – wild honey and locusts that were like grasshoppers.

God had given John a special job.

John told people, "You do a lot of bad things. You don't live as God would like you to live. Turn around and start doing what's right."

People asked him, "How can we make a fresh start?"

"Have you got two shirts?" John asked in reply. "If so, give one to somebody who doesn't have a shirt at all!"

John baptizes

Big crowds of people came to hear John.

"God wants to forgive you when you've done wrong," John told them. "Be baptized! That way, you can make a fresh start."

Many people said they were sorry for the wrong things they'd done. John baptized them in the River Jordan. He dipped them under the water. When they came out, they felt as if they had been born again.

People called him "John the Baptist".

In many different ways John preached the good news to the people.

Luke 3:18 CEV

Why did so many people come to listen to John?

Jesus is baptized

*As soon as Jesus
came out of the
water, he saw
the sky open
and the Holy
Spirit coming
down to him
like a dove.*

Mark 1:10 CEV

Some people came and asked John, "Are you the person God is sending to save us?"

"Someone much greater than me is coming," John said. "I'm not fit even to undo his sandals!"

Soon after, Jesus came to John.

"Please baptize me," said Jesus.

"But Jesus, *you* should be baptizing me," said John. "There's no way I should be baptizing you!"

"This is what God wants!" Jesus replied.

So John agreed. He dipped Jesus in the River Jordan.

When Jesus came out of the water, a voice from heaven said, "This is my own dear Son. I am very pleased with him!"

**Who was it
speaking after
Jesus was
baptized?**

293

Jesus in the desert

The Holy Spirit led Jesus into the desert, so that the devil could test him.

Matthew 4:1
CEV

After Jesus had been baptized, he went into the desert.
For forty days and nights he ate nothing.
Then the devil came to him.
"If you're really the Son of God, turn these stones into bread," said the devil.
Jesus answered, "The Bible says we don't live just by eating bread. We live by obeying every word that God says to us."

Jesus was tired and hungry when the devil came to test him.

Another test

"Don't try to
test the Lord
your God!"

Matthew 4:7
CEV

After this, the devil took Jesus
onto the roof of the Temple
in Jerusalem.

"Jump off!" said the devil.
"That will show everyone that you
are the Son of God. The Bible says
God's angels will stop you being hurt."

Jesus answered, "But the Bible also says we shouldn't
test God in such a stupid way!"

Did the devil leave Jesus now?

"Get out of here!"

The devil tried a third time.

He took Jesus to a very high mountain. From the top, they could see all the kingdoms of the world.

"I'll give you every one of these kingdoms to rule, if you kneel down and worship me," said the devil.

Jesus said, "Get out of here, Satan!"

At last the devil gave up and went away.

"The Scriptures say, 'You must worship the Lord your God; serve only him.'"

Matthew 4:10
NLT

Has the devil tempted you to do wrong things?

296

Jesus heals

The Jews had a special place to pray in most of their towns. This building was called a synagogue.

One time the people of Capernaum asked Jesus to speak in their synagogue. Afterward, a fisherman named Simon took Jesus home.

Simon's wife's mother wasn't feeling well. Jesus went to her bedside and told the illness to go. She felt better at once. She got up and cooked a meal for Jesus and his friends.

That evening many other sick people came and asked Jesus to heal them. He helped every one.

No matter what their diseases were, the touch of Jesus' hand healed every one.

Luke 4:40 NLT

Jesus was always ready to help people.

297

Jesus chooses a team

One day Jesus was standing by the shore of Lake Galilee. Lots of people crowded around him, listening to his wonderful stories.

Jesus noticed two fishing boats on the beach. The fishermen were washing their nets.

Jesus climbed into the boat that belonged to Simon.

"Push your boat out a little way from the shore," Jesus asked him.

Then Jesus spoke to the big crowd from the boat.

Jesus said, "People in other towns must hear the good news about God's kingdom. This is why I was sent."

Luke 4:43 CEV

Did he also help with the fishing?

Lots of fish

When he had finished teaching, Jesus said to Simon, "Push out into deeper water. Then let down your nets, so you can catch plenty of fish."

"But, Master," Simon replied, "we've been hard at work all night long – and we've not caught a single fish. However, if you say so, I'll let down the nets again."

This time the fishermen's nets were soon so full of fish that they began to rip. The men called to their friends in the other boat to help them. Before long, both boats were so full that they nearly sank.

Simon Peter and all who were with him were amazed at the catch of fish that they had taken.

Luke 5:9 NRSV

Jesus did many miracles with nature.

299

Fishing for people

Jesus told
Simon, "From
now on you will
bring in people
instead of fish."

Luke 5:10 CEV

Simon, his brother Andrew, and their fishermen friends, the twins James and John, were all astonished to see so many fish.

Simon went and knelt before Jesus.

"Leave me, Lord! I am sinful," said Simon.

"Don't be afraid!" Jesus told him. "From now on you will be fishing for people."

So the fishermen pulled their boats up the beach, left everything, and followed Jesus.

They became the first of Jesus' special friends, the "disciples".

Sometimes people also call Jesus' disciples his "apostles".

Jesus calls a taxman

People didn't like tax collectors. They swindled people and took too much money.

One day Jesus saw a taxman named Matthew working at his desk.

"Follow me!" Jesus called to him.

At once Matthew got up, left his work and his money, and followed Jesus. He became one of Jesus' disciples.

The twelve disciples were Peter (the new name Jesus gave Simon), Andrew (Peter's brother), James and his brother John, Philip, Bartholomew, Thomas, Matthew, another man also named James, Thaddaeus, Simon, and Judas Iscariot.

Jesus said, "I didn't come to invite good people to turn to God. I came to invite sinners."

Luke 5:32 CEV

Jesus chose twelve disciples – just as there were twelve tribes of Israel.

Wine for a wedding

One day a man invited Jesus to his wedding, in the village of Cana. Jesus' mother, Mary, went too – and Jesus' disciples.

Everyone was eating and drinking. Before long, they'd drunk all the wine. Now what could they drink?

"Fill those six big wine jars to the brim with water!" said Jesus.

The men did as Jesus told them.

Immediately the water was changed into wine.

"This is the best wine we've ever tasted!" people said.

Jesus made sure that wedding party went really well!

Jesus showed his glory, and his disciples put their faith in him.

John 2:11 CEV

Jesus enjoyed eating and drinking with his friends.

Born again!

A man named Nicodemus visited Jesus secretly, late one night.

"Teacher, I believe you have come from God," said Nicodemus.

"If you want to enter the kingdom of God," Jesus replied, "you must be born again."

"How can a grown-up be born again?" asked Nicodemus.

"This is a different kind of birth," Jesus said. "It's like being born into a new life."

"Please explain," said Nicodemus.

Jesus said, "God loved the world so much that he gave his only Son, so that anyone who believes in him shall not die, but live forever."

Everyone who has faith in the Son of Man will have eternal life.

John 3:15 CEV

Why do you think Nicodemus visited Jesus in secret?

Story
280

*Jesus said,
"No one who
drinks the
water I give will
ever be thirsty
again."*

John 4:14 CEV

People from
Samaria
were called
"Samaritans".
Jews and
Samaritans
had nothing to
do with each
other.

Living water

Jesus was feeling tired. He sat resting by a well in Samaria, when a woman came up with her water jar.

"Please give me a drink," said Jesus.

She was very surprised.

"You Jews don't usually speak to us people from Samaria," she said.

"If you knew who I am," Jesus said, "you would ask me for living water!"

"Living water?" she repeated. "What's that? You don't even have a bucket! How can you give me water?"

"Water from the well leaves you thirsty," Jesus replied. "But the water I give lasts forever."

"Then give me some," she said.

The woman was amazed by what Jesus said.

She shouted to her friends to come and meet him too.

A sick boy healed

An official from Capernaum begged Jesus to help him.

"My little boy is very sick. I think he might die," he said. "Please – come and heal him before it's too late!"

"Go back home," said Jesus. "Your son has been healed!"

The man believed Jesus and started walking home.

As he got near, servants rushed out to meet him.

"Master, the best news!" they said, smiling. "Your son has recovered!"

The happy father asked, "When did he start getting better?"

"About one o'clock yesterday afternoon," they said.

That was exactly the time Jesus told him his son was healed!

The man and everyone in his family put their faith in Jesus.

John 4:53 CEV

This official really believed that Jesus could help him.

Jesus saw how much faith they had.

Luke 5:20 CEV

Imagine if someone made a hole in the roof of your house and let down a sick person!

Through the roof!

A man who couldn't walk wanted Jesus to heal him. So four of his friends carried him on a stretcher to the house where Jesus was teaching.

When they saw the huge crowds there, they lifted the stretcher onto the flat roof of the house. Then they tore a hole in the roof and lowered the stretcher down in front of Jesus.

Stand up!

Jesus said to the man, "I forgive your sins."

Some of the religious leaders said, "Who does he think he is? Only God can forgive sin."

"Which is harder – to forgive sin or to heal sickness?" asked Jesus. "I can do both!"

Then Jesus said to the man, "Stand up! You are well."

The man jumped to his feet, picked up his stretcher, and hurried home.

Everyone was amazed and gave praise to God.

Luke 5:26 NIV

Do you think this man's friends believed Jesus could heal him?

*"God blesses
those people
whose hearts
are pure. They
will see him!"*

Matthew 5:8 CEV

Jesus' way

Jesus often went to the hills around the Sea of Galilee. One day a crowd followed him, to hear him teaching and telling stories.

Jesus explained about the good things God gives us.

"God blesses those people who trust only in him," he said. "God blesses people who are humble.

"Happy are people who want to do God's wishes.

"Forgive other people and you will be forgiven.

"People who work for peace shall be called God's children.

"Be happy; you will have a great reward in heaven."

Sometimes people call these sayings of Jesus the "Sermon on the Mount".

Stop the rot

Jesus often used everyday things to help people understand his teachings more easily.

"You are like salt that we put in our food to stop it rotting," he said. "You keep God's world from going bad.

"God says, 'You shall not murder.' But it's also wrong to get so angry that you want to murder someone.

"God says, 'Love your enemies and show kindness to those who do wrong to us.'"

"Make your light shine, so others will see the good you do and praise your Father in heaven."

Matthew 5:16
CEV

Jesus wanted to show us how we can live better lives.

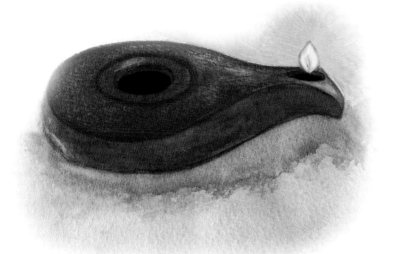

309

We often call this prayer "The Lord's Prayer".

How to pray

One of Jesus' friends asked him,
"Lord, how should we pray?"
    So Jesus taught them how to pray.
    "Go somewhere quiet when you want to pray
to God. He knows exactly what you need.
This is how you should pray to him:

"Our Father in heaven,
May your holy name be respected;
May your kingdom come;
May your will be done on earth,
    as it is in heaven.
Give us today the food we need.
Forgive us the wrongs we have done,
As we forgive the wrongs
    that others have done to us.
Do not bring us to the point of temptation,
But keep us safe from evil."

Based on Matthew 6:9–13 GNB

Jesus sends his team

Jesus sent out his twelve disciples to teach and preach.

He made them able to heal the sick.

They could even raise people from the dead!

Jesus said, "Not everyone will receive you kindly. Don't take with you any money, food, extra clothing, or shoes.

"God feeds the sparrows – and you're much more important than sparrows. So you can be sure God will give you everything you need."

Do you think everyone was pleased to see the disciples? Why?

The apostles left and went from village to village, telling the good news and healing people everywhere.

Luke 9:6 CEV

311

Two house builders

Jesus told this story.

Once two men each decided to build a house.

The first man found a sandy place, with a stream gurgling past.

"This is a great place for my house!" he said.

So he started to build his house on the sand. He was soon finished.

The second man searched for the best place for his house. He found some hard rock that suited well, and started to build. The walls grew tall, until finally he was finished.

*What
happened to
the two houses?*

312

Collapse!

Almost at once black clouds appeared.
Rain fell, winds blew, lightning flashed,
and thunder roared.

    CRRRAASHH!!! The first
man's house fell flat! The
man who built on the sand
was left with – nothing!

    But, despite the rain,
the second house stood
firm on the rock.

*Jesus said,
"Anyone who
hears what I
say and doesn't
obey me is like
someone whose
house wasn't
built on solid
rock."*

Luke 6:49 CEV

*How do you
think the man
who built on
sand felt?*

313

Riches

Here's another of Jesus' stories.

One year a farmer had such good crops that he became very rich.

His barns were full, so he built bigger ones. The farmer thought he had so much money he never need worry about anything again!

But God warned him:

"You're a fool! Tonight you will die – then what will become of all your money?"

Jesus explained, "Don't waste time worrying about money, clothes, or food. Birds don't plant crops and build barns – yet God provides food for them. Aren't you more valuable to God than the birds?"

Sometimes people say, "People matter more than things."

Sowing seed

Jesus told many stories that teach us a lesson. Here's another of them.

A farmer went out to plant seed. Some seed fell on the path. People walked on it, and birds flew down and ate it.

Some of the seed fell on rocky soil. It started to grow, but there wasn't enough soil to feed the roots, so the green shoots soon died.

Some seed fell among weeds. The weeds were too strong, and the seedlings died.

Some seed fell on good, rich soil. It grew tall and strong. At harvest time, the farmer harvested a hundred times more than he had planted!

Jesus said, "If you have ears, pay attention."

Mark 4:9 CEV

Jesus' special stories – the ones that teach us a lesson – are often called "parables".

*"What the
farmer is
spreading
is really the
message about
the kingdom."*

Mark 4:14 CEV

After Jesus had
told a parable,
he often
explained it to
his disciples.

Good fruit

The disciples asked Jesus what the story about the farmer planting seed meant.

"The seeds are God's words," Jesus explained. "Some of God's messages come to hard hearts, and the devil steals them away.

"Some of God's messages come to shallow hearts. People believe for a while, but then they lose interest.

"Some people's hearts are like a weed patch – other things come along and crowd out God's truth.

"But some people are like rich soil. They listen and believe God's words. His message grows and produces good things!"

Asleep in a boat

Jesus was with his disciples beside Lake Galilee.
He had been telling some of his wonderful stories.
Many people had come to listen.

When evening came, Jesus said to his friends,
"Let's go across to the other side of the lake."

So Jesus and his disciples said goodbye to the people
who'd been listening, and got into their boat. They set
sail across the lake.

Jesus felt very tired. He laid his head on a pillow
and fell asleep.

Suddenly, a strong wind blew down from the hills.
The little boat was caught in a fierce storm.

*A great gale
arose, and the
waves beat into
the boat.*

Mark 4:37 NRSV

*Did the boat
capsize in the
rough weather?*

317

*"Who is this?
Even the wind
and the waves
obey him!"*

Mark 4:41 CEV

Jesus showed
that he could
control even
the weather.

Stopping a storm

Hard rain fell. Waves tossed the boat backward and
forward. The disciples felt really scared.

But Jesus was still sleeping peacefully.

The disciples woke him.

"Master!" they shouted. "Please do something
to save us – we're all going to drown!"

Jesus stood up.

"Be still!" he said sternly to the wind
and the waves.

At that moment, the wind
dropped. The waves calmed.
Everything was still again.

"Why were you so
frightened?" asked Jesus.
"I am with you.
You can always
trust me."

A girl falls ill

Jairus fell at Jesus' feet and begged him to come to his house.

Luke 8:41 NRSV

A man named Jairus lived beside the Lake of Galilee. One day his little girl woke up feeling quite ill.

Jairus was worried.

He knew that Jesus healed people, so he went off to find him.

"Please come to see my little girl," Jairus asked.

"I'll come at once," said Jesus.

Jairus was in charge of the synagogue in Capernaum.

Bad news

They set off together. Then Jairus saw a man pushing through the crowd.

"Don't bother Jesus now," said the messenger. "Your little girl has died."

"Don't be scared!" Jesus said gently to Jairus. "Just believe in me."

Jesus walked on with Jairus.

Jesus went into Jairus's house, taking just his close friends, James, Peter, and John.

*Jesus said,
"Have faith,
and your
daughter will
get well."*

Luke 8:50 CEV

**Was Jesus able
to help Jairus's
daughter?**

Story
297

Her parents
were
astounded.

Luke 8:56 REB

Jesus told
Jairus and his
wife to have
faith that their
little girl would
get well.

Wake up!

As soon as they got inside the house, they heard lots of weeping and wailing.

"Please go away!" said Jesus to the people making all the noise. "The little girl isn't dead – she's asleep."

They laughed at him.

Jesus sent them off and then followed Jairus into the room where the girl lay.

Jesus took her hand gently in his warm hands.

"My dear, wake up!" he said.

The girl opened her eyes. Then she sat up and looked around. "Find your daughter something to eat," said Jesus. Very soon she was feeling much better.

No shops!

Jesus was tired and went to the hills for a rest. He saw a crowd of people gathering and felt sorry for them.

Jesus placed his hands on everyone who was ill and talked to them. Suddenly, they were well. They could see, they could walk and run again! They all went away, thanking God.

After this, Jesus sat down and started to tell the crowd some of his wonderful stories.

The day went on, and before long, the sun began to set.

By now people were feeling tired and hungry. They hadn't brought food with them – and there were no shops in the hills.

Jesus felt sorry for them and healed everyone who was sick.

Matthew 14:14
CEV

How did this huge crowd find enough to eat?

"We have only
five loaves of
bread and two
fish!"

Matthew 14:17
NLT

How could that
be enough for
everyone?

A boy's lunch

"Master!" said the disciples. "Shall we
send the people away to a village to buy bread?"

"No – we must feed them here," said Jesus.

So Jesus' friends went around the hillside, asking,
"Has anyone brought food with them?"
Everyone shook their heads.

"I have a little bread," said one boy at last.
"And two small fish. Jesus can have them!"

A disciple led the boy to Jesus.

"Master!" he said. "Here's a boy with five loaves
and two fish."

Jesus smiled at the boy and took his basket.

"Tell everyone to sit down," Jesus told
his friends.

Jesus asked
God's blessing
on the food.

Matthew 14:19
NLT

What do you
think the little
boy told his
mother when
he got home?

Plenty for all!

Jesus took the loaves from the boy's basket and broke them. Then he gave the bread to his friends. Next Jesus divided up the little fish and gave pieces to his friends.

The disciples started giving the food to the crowd. Jesus went on breaking up the bread and fish and giving out more.

More than five thousand people were sitting on the hillside – and everyone had plenty to eat.

When they had all eaten, Jesus asked his friends to pick up the leftovers. There were twelve baskets full of scraps. It was a wonderful miracle!

Walking on water

Jesus had climbed a mountain to pray on his own. The disciples waited. But Jesus didn't come, so they got in their boat and sailed off to Capernaum.

A storm arose suddenly.

Then the disciples saw someone walking on the lake. Was it a ghost? They felt terrified.

It was Jesus! He called out to them.

"If it's really you," said Peter, "let me walk on the water as well."

"Come on then!" said Jesus.

Peter started to walk on the water. But after a few steps, he got frightened and started to sink.

Jesus reached out and held him up.

They both climbed into the boat – and the storm stopped.

"You don't have much faith," Jesus said. *"Why did you doubt me?"*

Matthew 14:31
NLT

Why couldn't Peter walk very far on the water?

327

The man's eyes
were healed,
and he saw
everything
clearly.

Mark 8:25 CEV

Jesus healed
this man near
the village of
Bethsaida.

Trees walking!

Some people brought a blind man to Jesus.
"Please give him sight!" they asked.

Jesus put some spit on the man's eyes,
then covered them with his hands.

He took his hands away and asked,
"Can you see now?"

"Yes! I can see shapes," said the man.
"But people look like trees walking around!"

Jesus put his hands on the man's eyes again.

This time the man could see everything clearly.

Dangerous journey

Here is one of Jesus' best-loved stories.

Once a man had to travel from Jerusalem to Jericho, along a lonely road through the mountains. Robbers stole everything he had and beat him up. Then they ran off, leaving him lying injured.

A priest was walking to Jerusalem. When he noticed the man on the ground, he just crossed to the other side of the road and walked on.

Along came a man who helped in the Temple. As soon as he saw the injured man, he crossed over and walked past.

An expert in the Law stood up to test Jesus. "Teacher," he asked, "what must I do to inherit eternal life?"

Luke 10:25 NIV

People often call this the story of "The Good Samaritan".

329

Jesus said, "Go
and do the
same!"

Luke 10:37 CEV

**Does Jesus
want us to help
only people we
know?**

A stranger helps

A third man came along. He was a foreigner,
from the land of Samaria.

But he stopped and bandaged the man's wounds.
Then he helped him onto his donkey, and took him
to an inn.

"Look after my friend!" he told the innkeeper.
"Make sure he has everything he needs."

"Which of the three men
acted like a true friend
to the man who was
robbed?" asked Jesus.

"The stranger," came
the answer.

"Yes: the stranger did
exactly what God wants."

Two sisters

Jesus had friends who lived in the village of Bethany. There were two sisters, Mary and Martha, and their brother, Lazarus.

One day Jesus came for a visit. Martha started to prepare a special meal for him.

She asked her sister to help her. But Mary wanted to sit and listen to Jesus.

Martha got quite angry.

"Tell my sister to give me a hand with the cooking," said Martha.

But Jesus said, "Learning about God is more important than food."

Story
305

"Mary has chosen what is best, and it will not be taken away from her."

Luke 10:42 CEV

Would you have been angry with Mary, like Martha?

331

Jesus said,
"I am the one
who raises the
dead to life!"

John 11:25 CEV

Jesus is late

One day Lazarus became sick.

Mary and Martha were afraid he might die.

They sent a message to Jesus.

"Please come and heal Lazarus," they asked.

But Jesus didn't rush to see them.

After a few days, he said to his disciples,
"Let's go now."

By the time Jesus reached Bethany, Lazarus was
dead.

"If you'd been here, Lazarus wouldn't have died,"
said Martha. "But even now, he will come back to life
if you tell him to."

Did Jesus arrive too late to help?

Come out!

"Take me to Lazarus's grave," said Jesus.

A great stone blocked the doorway to his tomb.

"Roll that stone away!" said Jesus.

Then he called, "Lazarus, come out of the grave!"

And Lazarus appeared!

People were astonished – and a bit frightened too.

Jesus said, "Now take off his burial clothes!"

Lazarus went home with his sisters. They were
so happy!

*Jesus started
crying, and
the people
said, "See how
much he loved
Lazarus."*

John 11:35–36
CEV

*Why might
Jesus have
decided not
to rush to
Bethany to heal
Lazarus?*

One grateful man

"Your faith has
made you well."

Luke 17:19 NLT

One time ten men with the terrible skin disease called leprosy came to Jesus.

They called out, "Master, have pity on us!"

"Go and show yourselves to the priest," he said.

People with leprosy had to do this if they thought their disease had gone. The priest had to check that they were really well again.

Do you always remember to thank God for all he has done for you?

As the ten men walked to the Temple, their skin became clear and healthy. One of them ran back to Jesus. "Praise God! I'm completely healed," he said.

"I healed ten men," said Jesus. "Where are the others? You are the only one who has come back to thank me."

A straight back

There was a woman whose back had been badly bent for many years. She couldn't stand up straight.

One day she went to the synagogue where Jesus was teaching. He felt sad that she was in pain.

"Your back is completely healed," Jesus told her.

As soon as he said this, she was able to stand up straight!

She was so happy! She gave thanks to God.

The people were delighted with all the wonderful things Jesus was doing.

Luke 13:17 NIV

Jesus healed this woman on the Sabbath. Some people thought it wrong to do so on the day of rest.

335

Lost sheep

Here is another of the much-loved stories Jesus told.

There was once a good shepherd, who had exactly one hundred sheep. He knew them all by name and loved every one of them.

One night a sheep went missing. The shepherd immediately set out in search of his lost sheep.

At last he found it. He carried the lost sheep home on his strong shoulders.

The shepherd called to his friends.

"Be happy!" he said. "I have found my lost sheep."

Jesus said, "I am like a good shepherd. I care for people who are lost."

"Your Father in heaven doesn't want any of these little ones to be lost."

Matthew 18:14
CEV

Jesus said he came to seek out people who are lost.

A lost coin

This is another of Jesus' stories that has a hidden meaning.

A woman had ten silver coins, but she lost one of them in her house.

　She swept the floor carefully, searching every corner and every crack.

　At last she found the missing coin!

　She was so happy she had found her lost coin that she called in her friends to celebrate with her.

Jesus said, "In the same way, God's angels are happy when even one person turns to him."

Luke 15:10 CEV

The silver coins were probably given to the woman at her wedding.

337

Story
312

A boy leaves home

Jesus also told this great story.

There was once a rich farmer who had two sons.

One day the younger son went to his father.

"Give me my share of your money," said the boy. "Then I can go off and enjoy myself."

The father felt sad. He loved having his sons at home.

But he gave the younger son his share of his money.

The boy left home and went away to a far country. He had a great time!

338

Greedy pigs

But one day the boy's money ran out.

It wasn't easy to find work – and there was no food.

The younger son went to a farmer.

"Give me something to eat," he said. "I'll work very hard for you."

"You can look after my pigs," said the farmer.

So the boy sat with the grunting, greedy pigs.

After a bit, he began thinking of his family at home.

"How stupid I've been!" he said to himself.

"There are lots of men working for my father. They have as much food as they need. Here am I, envying pigs their food! I'll go home and say, 'Father, I don't deserve to be called your son any more. Can I work for you to pay for my food?'"

Do you think his father took him back?

"So he got up and went to his father."

Luke 15:20 NIV

339

The welcoming father

Story
314

*Jesus said,
"In the same
way, there is
more happiness
in heaven
because of
one sinner
who turns to
God than over
ninety-nine
good people
who don't
need to."*

Luke 15:7 CEV

**God is always
ready to
forgive us.**

So the boy set out on the long walk home.

While he was still a good way off, his glad father ran to meet him. He hugged and kissed his son.

The boy started to speak the words he'd practised. "Dad, I'm so sorry…"

His father started to laugh.

"My son is home again!" he cried. "Bring out the best clothes for him. Bring him smart shoes! Cook a feast! I thought my son was dead – but he's home again. He was lost – now he's found. We'll have such a party!"

340

An angry brother

When the older son finished work in the fields,
he came home. He heard music and laughter.

"We're having a party for your young brother,"
a servant told him.

"I've always been a good son and a hard worker,"
the older son complained to his father. "You've never
given me a party! My brother has wasted your money.
Now he comes home – and you celebrate!"

"Don't be angry," said the father.
"Everything I have is yours!"

*"Your brother
was lost and
has now been
found."*

Luke 15:32 CEV

***Why was the
older brother
so angry?***

341

Jesus loves children

One day some mothers brought their children to Jesus. His disciples started sending them away.

"Jesus is very tired," they said. "Don't pester him with your kids!"

Jesus heard what they were saying.

"Let the little children come to me!" he said. "Don't stop them! You must love God like a little child if you want to enter heaven."

Then Jesus picked up the children and held them in his arms.

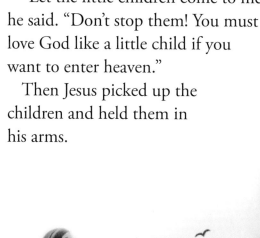

A blind man sees

A blind man named Bartimaeus lived near the city of Jericho. He heard that Jesus was coming, and knew that he healed people.

So Bartimaeus sat by the road, shouting, "Jesus, have mercy on me!"

People around him got annoyed.

"Do be quiet, Bartimaeus!" they said.

He called out louder, "Please, Jesus, help me!"

Jesus heard.

"What do you want?" Jesus asked.

"Teacher, I want you to give me my sight!"

"It's done!" said Jesus.

"Your faith has healed you."

From that moment, Bartimaeus could see perfectly!

When all the people saw it, they also praised God.

Luke 18:43 NIV

Did Bartimaeus believe that Jesus could heal him?

Man up a tree

Story
318

Zacchaeus was a chief tax collector and was very wealthy.

Luke 19:2 NIV

Zacchaeus probably thought he wouldn't be noticed if he sat in the tree.

In Jericho, there also lived a man named Zacchaeus. He was the chief tax collector. Zacchaeus grew very rich, because he took more money than he was supposed to.

"He's a thief!" people said. No one liked him.

Jesus was visiting Jericho. Everyone crowded the streets to see him.

Zacchaeus wanted to see Jesus too, but he was very short.

He clambered up a sycamore tree and sat on a high branch. Now he would see Jesus too!

A big change!

Jesus said,
"The Son of
Man came to
seek and to save
what was lost."

Luke 19:10 NIV

Jesus gives
people a fresh
start when they
come to him.

Zacchaeus had a big shock.
When Jesus reached his tree,
he stopped.

"Zacchaeus," Jesus called,
"come down! I want to have
dinner with you today!"

Zacchaeus was astonished. He slithered down
the tree.

After Zacchaeus met Jesus, he changed. He became
much kinder.

"I'll give half my money to poor people,"
Zacchaeus said. "I'm going to put right all the wrong
I've done."

"God is so pleased you're making a fresh start,"
said Jesus.

Jesus' last Passover

It was the time of the great festival called Passover.

Jesus decided to go to Jerusalem for the feast with his twelve disciples.

On their way Jesus said to his friends, "I'm going to be taken prisoner and killed in Jerusalem. But after three days, I will be raised from the dead."

The disciples didn't understand what he was talking about.

We will soon find out what Jesus meant.

A borrowed donkey

When they arrived near Bethany, just outside Jerusalem, Jesus sent off two of his friends.

"Go into the next village," he told them. "You'll find a donkey tied up. Nobody has ever ridden it. Untie the donkey and bring it to me. If anyone asks what you're doing, say, 'The master needs the donkey!'"

The two disciples found the donkey easily. They untied it and brought it to Jesus. Some of Jesus' friends spread their cloaks over the donkey's back.

"The Lord needs it."

Luke 19:34 NLT

Jesus' friends – Mary, Martha, and Lazarus – lived in Bethany.

347

Years before,
the wise men
had realized
that a new
king had been
born. Now the
people saw that
Jesus was king.

Jesus the king

Jesus sat on the young donkey and rode into Jerusalem. The road was filled with people coming to the city for the great festival.

When the crowds saw Jesus coming, they grew very excited. Some welcomed Jesus as king, spreading out their cloaks on the road before him.

Others cut down branches from palm trees and laid them on the road.

People started shouting with joy.

Soon everyone joined in, chanting: "Hosanna! Hooray for God!" and "Praise God in heaven!"

The priests' plot

Judas said, "What will you give me if I betray Jesus to you?"

*Matthew 26:15
NRSV*

Some of the priests from the Temple hated Jesus. They were plotting to kill him.

Judas Iscariot, one of Jesus' disciples, went to see the chief priests.

"If you pay me well," he said, "I will show you where you can find Jesus and arrest him easily."

The priests were delighted. They promised to pay Judas thirty silver coins for doing this.

Judas waited for a good time to hand Jesus over to them.

When would that be?

Jesus gets angry

When they arrived in Jerusalem, Jesus and his disciples went first to the Temple.

Jesus saw that many shopkeepers had set up tables there. They were selling things and changing money.

Jesus was very angry.

"You've made God's Temple into a den of thieves!" he shouted.

Jesus chased the men who were buying and selling right out of the Temple.
He threw over their tables
and upset their stalls.

"My house shall be called a house of prayer for all the nations. But you have made it a den of robbers."

Mark 11:17
NRSV

Did it surprise you that Jesus got angry with these people?

351

Jesus wanted to teach his disciples as much as possible before he left them.

Sheep and goats

One day Jesus explained to his disciples how he would choose people for his kingdom.

"I will come back to the earth in glory. Everyone will stand before me. I will be like a shepherd, separating the sheep from the goats.

"I'll say to the sheep, 'Come into my kingdom. When I was hungry, you fed me. When I was thirsty, you gave me something to drink. When I was a stranger, you invited me into your homes. And when I was sick or in prison, you visited me.'

"They will say, 'Lord, we don't remember doing those things for you.'

"And I will say, 'When you cared for any needy people, it was as if you were caring for me.'"

The broken jar

One evening Jesus' friends in Bethany held a special dinner for him.

Mary came in with a jar of precious perfume. She broke the jar and poured the perfume over Jesus' feet. Then she dried his feet with her long hair.

Judas Iscariot was shocked.

"Master!" he said. "A big jar of perfume like that should be sold. We could use the money to help many poor people."

"Don't protest about what Mary has done," said Jesus. "She showed her love for me in a beautiful way."

Jesus said, "Wherever the good news is preached throughout the world, this woman's deed will be talked about."

Matthew 26:13
NLT

Why was Judas so shocked?

Follow that man!

The day of the great feast had come. Jesus wanted to celebrate Passover with his twelve special friends.

The disciples asked Jesus where they should prepare the meal.

"Walk to the edge of the city. You will see a man carrying a big jug of water," said Jesus. "Follow him home. Then say, 'Please show us the room you have prepared for the master.' He will show you a room that is all ready for Passover."

The disciples did as Jesus told them. Later Jesus and the others arrived for the meal.

Jesus said, "I will not eat another Passover meal until it is finally eaten in God's kingdom."

Luke 22:16 CEV

Jesus celebrated Passover in a large upstairs room.

Washing feet

When they had all gathered, Jesus asked his friends, "Who is greater: the master or the servant?"

They said, "The master, of course!"

"Well, I'm the master of this feast," said Jesus. "But I'm also your servant."

Then he took a bowl of water and washed his disciples' feet. He dried them with a towel.

"I, your master, have washed your feet," said Jesus. "Think how important it is for you to wash each other's feet!"

Jesus said, "I have given you an example so that you may copy what I have done to you."

John 13:15 NJB

In Bible lands, a host always provided water to wash the dusty feet of his guests.

Love one another

As they were eating, Jesus said, "One of you eating this meal with me is going to hand me over to my enemies."

The disciples felt scared.

"Jesus, surely you don't mean me!" said some.

"I'm talking about someone who's dipping into the same bowl of food as me," he said.

Just then Judas crept out. He was plotting against Jesus. "Love one another, as I have loved you," Jesus told his disciples.

Who do you think Judas was meeting?

Bread and wine

Jesus took some bread. He thanked God for it. Then he broke it and gave a piece to each of his friends.

Jesus said, "Take this bread and eat it! I am the bread. I am giving myself for all of you."

Then Jesus took a cup of wine. He thanked God for it.

Then Jesus passed the cup to his disciples. "Drink some of this wine!" he said. "The wine is my life. I offer my life for all."

The disciples drank the wine.

He took a loaf of bread... and gave it to them, saying, "This is my body, which is given for you."

Luke 22:19 NRSV

Christians share bread and wine at a meeting called communion to remember Jesus' life and death.

358

*Jesus said,
"I am the way,
the truth, and
the life!"*

John 14:6 CEV

Peter's warning

"I love you so much
that I would even
die for you!"
Peter declared.
   Jesus shook his
head sadly.
   "Peter! Before
the rooster crows
tomorrow morning,
you'll say three
times you don't
even know me!"

*What was
going to
happen?*

In the garden

After supper, Jesus took his disciples out of the city.

He led them to a garden called Gethsemane, on the Mount of Olives.

"Wait here for me," said Jesus. "I want to pray alone. Stay awake – and pray!"

Jesus chose three of his special friends – Peter, James, and John – to pray with him.

Jesus said to them, "I am so sad that I feel as if I am dying. Stay here and keep awake with me."

Matthew 26:38 CEV

Jesus knew that Judas was going to betray him. He felt very, very sad.

Story
333

*Jesus said,
"The time has
come for the
Son of Man to
be handed over
to sinners."*

Matthew 26:45
CEV

*How did Jesus
feel, when
he found
his disciples
sleeping?*

Asleep!

Jesus went a little further into the garden.
He knelt to pray. He was frightened about
what was going to happen.

"Father, don't let me have to do this!" he prayed.
"But it's not what I want that matters – it's what
you want. Let everything happen as you wish."

Jesus walked back to the three disciples.
They were all asleep.

"Peter!" Jesus said, waking him.
"Why are you sleeping? Couldn't
you pray with me for just one
hour? Please watch and pray!"
Jesus went alone into the
garden again to pray. But the
disciples went back
to sleep.

363

Judas kisses

"Wake up!" Jesus shouted to his friends. "Here comes the man who's going to hand me over to my enemies!"

Judas was leading some men carrying swords, sticks, and lanterns.

He had told the priests, "The man I kiss is the one you should arrest."

Now Judas walked right up to Jesus and kissed him. "Teacher!" he said.

So the men with Judas knew this was Jesus.

The guards seized Jesus and took him prisoner.

Deserted!

Peter was furious! He grabbed a sword and cut off the ear of the high priest's servant.

"Peter, put away that sword," Jesus told him.

Then Jesus healed the man's ear.

"You've come after me as if I was a thief," Jesus said to the men. "Why didn't you arrest me while I was teaching in the Temple?"

The disciples all ran off. They were very frightened.

Jesus said to the chief priests, "This is your hour – when darkness reigns."

Luke 22:52–53
REB

Now Jesus was alone with his enemies.

365

Peter hears the rooster

The soldiers took Jesus to the high priest's house.
Peter followed.

While they questioned Jesus inside,
Peter waited in the courtyard.

A servant girl said,
"I think I've seen that man with Jesus."

Peter was frightened.
"No! I don't even *know* him," he said.

A man looked across and said,
"Yes, that's one of Jesus' disciples."

"Honestly, I'm not!" said Peter.

A third man said, "He *must* be one of Jesus' people."

"I have nothing to do with this man Jesus!"
shouted Peter.

As he spoke, soldiers led Jesus
across the courtyard.
Jesus looked at Peter.

A rooster crowed!

Then Peter remembered
that Jesus had told him,
"You will say you don't
know me three times before
the rooster crows."

Peter had
been one of
Jesus' boldest
friends; now
he was so
scared he said
he didn't even
know Jesus.

The priests' questions

Jesus stood before the high priest, who had called in the other priests.

"Are you the king whom God has sent?" asked the high priest. "Are you the Son of God?"

"Yes," Jesus answered, "I am."

"Do you hear that?" the priests shouted angrily. "He says he's the Son of God!"

They all thought Jesus should die.

The soldiers made fun of him, spat on him, and hit him.

"Soon you will see the Son of Man sitting at the right side of God All-Powerful and coming on the clouds of heaven."

Matthew 26:64
CEV

Jesus suffered even more later.

*Jesus told
Pilate, "I was
born into
this world to
tell about the
truth."*

John 18:37 CEV

The priests
could not have
Jesus put to
death: only
Pilate could do
that.

Pilate's question

The soldiers took Jesus to the Roman ruler,
Pontius Pilate.

"This man Jesus is causing a great deal of trouble,"
the priests told Pilate. "He even says he's the king
of the Jews. You should have him put to death!"

Pilate questioned Jesus carefully.

"I can find nothing wrong with him," said Pilate,
when he had finished.

Then he asked Jesus,
"Are you the king of
the Jews?"

"Those are your
words," Jesus
answered.

To the cross!

Now Pilate sent Jesus to King Herod.

Herod spoke to Jesus, but Jesus wouldn't answer. Finally Herod gave up. His soldiers mocked Jesus, then marched him back to Pilate.

"This man has done nothing he should die for," said Pilate.

Each year at Passover, he set one prisoner free.

"Who shall I free – Jesus or the murderer Barabbas?" Pilate asked the crowd.

"Barabbas! Let Barabbas go free!" they yelled.

"What shall I do with Jesus?" asked Pilate.

"Put him on the cross!" they all screamed.

Pilate called for a bowl of water. In front of everyone, he washed his hands.

"Have your way! Take him and crucify him. But don't blame me for Jesus' death."

Then Pilate handed Jesus over to be nailed to a cross.

John 19:16 CEV

Do you think Pilate was wise or cowardly?

369

Judas is very sorry

"I have sinned,"
Judas declared,
"for I have
betrayed an
innocent man."

Matthew 27:4
NLT

Can you
imagine how
guilty Judas
felt?

Judas felt dreadfully sorry for what he had done.
He took back the thirty pieces of silver
to the priests who had paid him.
"I don't want your money!" he said.
"I've done wrong. I betrayed the Lord."
They laughed.
"That's tough! It's too late now!"
Judas flung the money on the floor.
He was so sad he had
turned against Jesus
that he took his
own life.

Three crosses

Finally Roman soldiers marched Jesus away. They took him outside Jerusalem. Guards forced him to carry a heavy, wooden cross up a hill.

When Jesus stumbled, soldiers made a man from the crowd carry it for him.

On the hill they fixed Jesus on the cross. They also put two robbers on crosses, one each side of Jesus.

"Please remember me!" one robber asked Jesus.

"Today you will be with me in heaven," said Jesus.

Pilate told the soldiers to nail a sign over Jesus' head. It said: "Jesus of Nazareth, the king of the Jews."

Why do you think Pilate wanted this notice on the cross?

Jesus said, "Father, forgive them, for they do not know what they are doing."

Luke 23:34 NIV

Jesus dies

Jesus' family and his friends stood sadly near the cross.

"Treat my mother Mary as if she were your own mother," Jesus told his friend John.

Jesus was very lonely as he died.

"God, why have you left me?" he asked.

The sky went dark from midday till three o'clock.

Jesus cried out, "It is finished!"

Then he died.

A Roman captain said,

"That really *was*

God's Son!"

Even when
he was dying,
Jesus showed
his love for his
mother, Mary.

Joseph's request

After Jesus died, a good man named Joseph went to Pilate.

"Jesus is dead now," he said. "May I look after his body?"

Pilate nodded, "You may!"

So Joseph took Jesus' body and wrapped it in a cloth. Then he laid it in a grave carved from rock. Finally Joseph rolled a huge stone across the doorway of the grave, so that Jesus' body would not be disturbed.

Two Roman soldiers stood guard at the door.

Mary Magdalene and Mary, the mother of Jesus, were watching and saw where the body was placed.

Mark 15:47 CEV

Now no one could enter the tomb!

373

*The apostles
thought it was
all nonsense,
and they would
not believe.*

Luke 24:11 CEV

Mary's discovery

Early Sunday morning, while it was still dark,
Mary Magdalene went to Jesus' tomb.
(Jesus had healed this Mary when he was preaching
in Galilee.) Mary was taking perfume to put
on Jesus' body.

   Mary was astonished to see that the
great stone in front of the door had
been rolled back. But she could not
see Jesus' body!

   Mary rushed back into
Jerusalem.

   "They've taken away Jesus'
body," she said to Peter
and John. "I can't find it!"

**What had
happened to
Jesus' body?**

375

Risen!

*Till this
moment they
had still not
understood the
Scripture, that
he must rise
from the dead.*

John 20:9 NJB

*Why did Peter
and John now
believe Jesus
had risen from
the dead?*

Peter and John were very concerned. They decided to see for themselves and rushed off to the tomb.

John arrived first, because he could run faster than Peter. He bent down at the door, and peered in.

Peter arrived, all out of breath. He dashed right into the tomb. There was no body!

The sheets that Jesus' body had been wrapped in were now neatly folded.

Immediately Peter and John believed that Jesus had risen from the dead.

The gardener?

Peter and John went back into Jerusalem.

But Mary stayed outside the tomb, crying.
She peered into the tomb again. Through her tears,
she saw two angels.

"Why are you crying?" they asked her.

"They've taken away Jesus' body," she answered.
"I don't know where it is."

Mary turned around and saw Jesus standing there –
but she didn't recognize him.

"Why are you crying?"
Jesus asked Mary. "Who are
you looking for?"

Mary thought it was the
gardener, so she said,
"If you've taken Jesus' body,
please tell me where you've
put it."

Jesus said, "Mary!"

Immediately Mary knew
he was Jesus.

"Teacher!" she said.

*Mary
Magdalene
went to the
disciples with
the news:
"I have seen
the Lord!"*

John 20:18 NIV

**How did Mary
Magdalene
recognize Jesus?**

Two sad friends

Jesus explained to them everything written about himself in the Scriptures.

Luke 24:27 CEV

Two of Jesus' followers were walking to Emmaus, a village near Jerusalem. They had heard some disciples say that they'd seen Jesus alive again. But these two still thought Jesus was dead.

Suddenly, a stranger appeared on the road and started walking with them. It was Jesus – but the men didn't recognize him.

"What are you talking about?" asked Jesus.

One of them said, "You must be the only person who doesn't know what's happened in Jerusalem."

"What?" asked Jesus.

"Jesus of Nazareth has been put to death...

Why do you think these followers of Jesus didn't believe he was alive again?

Some women amazed us, saying they couldn't find Jesus' body when they visited his tomb this morning."

A stranger to supper

As they approached their village, the men said,
"Stay with us. It's evening; soon it will be dark."

So Jesus sat down to supper with them. He thanked
God for the food. Then he broke the bread and gave
some to each of the men.

Suddenly, they saw that the stranger was Jesus!
At that very moment, he disappeared.

"*It was Jesus!*" said one of them. "Didn't you feel
excited when he explained the Bible to us,
as we were walking along?"

They jumped up and
rushed straight back
to Jerusalem.

They found Jesus'
eleven disciples.

"It's all true!"
they said. "Jesus
really *is* alive!
We've seen him
with our own
eyes!"

*Their eyes were
opened and
they recognized
him.*

Luke 24:31 NIV

**When did
these disciples
recognize Jesus?**

Friends go fishing

Jesus said to
Simon Peter,
"Take care of
my sheep."

John 21:16 NIV

Peter and some of the other disciples went fishing
again. They fished all night, but didn't catch anything.
At sunrise, they saw someone on the shore.

"How's the fishing?" called the stranger.

"We haven't caught anything!"

"Throw the nets on the other side of the boat,"
suggested the stranger.

They did so, and immediately the
nets were so full of fish that the
men couldn't pull them in.

*Who was the
stranger?*

"It must be Jesus!" shouted John.
Peter was so glad to see Jesus that he swam ashore.
Jesus cooked some of the fish for them over a fire.

Always!

Story
350

*Jesus said, "Go
to the people of
all nations and
make them my
disciples."*

Matthew 28:19
CEV

The disciple
Thomas didn't
believe Jesus
was alive
until he met
him and saw
his wounded
hands.

Forty days after Easter, Jesus' disciples were in a house in Jerusalem. Suddenly, Jesus appeared in the middle of the room. At first they were scared.

"Don't be afraid!" said Jesus. "Men killed me – but God has brought me back to life."

"Will you now become king of the world?" asked the disciples.

"No – not yet," said Jesus. "A lot has to happen before that."

After this, Jesus walked with them to the Mount of Olives, just outside Jerusalem.

As they were standing with Jesus on the hill, he said, "Now I'm going to be with God. But I am still with you. I will always be with you."

382

Jesus goes away

Jesus said to
them... "The
Holy Spirit will
come upon you
and give you
power."

Acts 1:7–8 CEV

Then, as Jesus was
talking to them, a cloud
came down from the sky. It took
Jesus away.

When the cloud disappeared, the disciples
couldn't see Jesus any more.

They stood staring into the sky.

Suddenly, two angels appeared.

"Why are you all staring up at the sky?" asked the
angels. "Jesus is with God in heaven. One day he will
return. Now do as Jesus told you."

So the disciples walked back into Jerusalem,
very happy. They went to the Temple and thanked
God for everything that had happened.

Before he left
them, Jesus
had told his
disciples
to take his
message to
every part of
the world.

Better than money!

There was a man in Jerusalem who had been disabled all his life. Each day friends carried him to the gate of the Temple. He sat there, begging.

One morning Peter and John passed him as they were going to the Temple to pray.

"Can you spare me a few coins?" he asked.

"I have no money," said Peter. "But I can give you something better. In Jesus' name, get up and walk!"

Right away the man jumped up, shouting praises to God. Everyone who saw it was amazed.

The disciples continued to heal people and do miracles.

Don't preach!

*Peter and
John said...
"We cannot
keep quiet
about what we
have seen and
heard."*

Acts 4:19–20
CEV

The priests
arrested Peter and
John for preaching about
Jesus. They put them
both in prison. But after
questioning them, the priests
let them go. Healing people
wasn't against the law!

But they told Peter and John,
"You must *not* preach about Jesus again."

Peter and John said, "Jesus told us to preach.
Should we obey humans or God?"

Did they stop preaching?

Philip...
explained the
good news
about Jesus.

Acts 8:35 CEV

The disciples
baptized
people after
they trusted in
Jesus.

Philip helps an African

Believers talked about Jesus wherever they went.

One day, as Philip was on the road, he met a man from Africa riding a chariot. The man was reading the Bible, but looked confused. He didn't understand what he was reading.

Philip explained the Scriptures and told the man about Jesus.

"Why can't I be baptized?" asked the man.

"You can," said Philip, "if you truly believe."

"I believe Jesus is the Son of God," said the African.

So Philip baptized him in a stream.

Saul meets Jesus

In Jerusalem lived a Jewish man named Saul. He hated the followers of Jesus.

Saul wanted to go to Damascus, to search out believers and arrest them. He took some soldiers with him to help.

On his way there a brilliant light suddenly shone down. A voice said, "Saul, I am Jesus. Why are you trying to harm me?"

Saul fell to the ground. He was blinded!

"What shall I do, Lord?" asked Saul, in fear.

"Go to Damascus and you will be told what to do," said the Lord.

"Saul, Saul, why are you persecuting me?"

Acts 9:5 NJB

Who spoke to Saul on his way to Damascus?

387

Saul becomes Paul

Soon Saul...
started telling
people that
Jesus is the Son
of God.

Acts 9:20 CEV

Ananias was
brave to meet
Saul, when he
knew Saul had
been arresting
believers.

In Damascus there lived a believer named Ananias.

"Go to a house in Straight Street!" God told him. "There you'll find a man named Saul. I want you to help him."

"But I'm afraid!" said Ananias. "This man Saul has been arresting the followers of Jesus!"

"He's now a changed man," God told Ananias. "I've chosen Saul to tell the good news about Jesus!"

So Ananias went to find Saul. He prayed with him, and God gave Saul back his sight.

From that time on, Saul followed Jesus. And he changed his name from Saul to Paul!

Unchained!

While Peter was being kept in jail, the church never stopped praying to God for him.

Acts 12:5 CEV

See how many other stories you can remember in which angels helped people.

Now King Herod started to get tough with believers in Jesus. He killed John's brother, James. He put Peter in jail. Herod planned to kill him too.

The believers prayed hard for Peter.

It was the night before he was to be executed. Peter was asleep in prison, chained between two soldiers.

An angel appeared and woke Peter.

"Get up quickly!" said the angel.

The chains fell off Peter's arms.

"Now get dressed!" said the angel.

Open the door!

The angel led Peter out through the prison gates – which opened by themselves!

Then the angel disappeared.

Peter hurried to the house where the believers were praying. He knocked at the door.

A girl named Rhoda came to answer. When she heard his voice, she ran back inside, shouting, "Peter's here!"

"Impossible!" they said. "It must be his angel!"

But Peter kept knocking – until finally they came and let him in.

Peter said, "The Lord has sent his angel and saved me from Herod."

Acts 12:11 NLT

Peter must have been worried that soldiers might catch him again, while he was waiting outside the door!

Paul travels

A believer named Barnabas asked Paul to help preach the good news about Jesus to people. They visited towns in Cyprus and Turkey, telling people about Jesus.

When Paul and Barnabas preached, they often upset Jews who didn't believe in Jesus.

If a group of people did believe in Jesus, Paul and Barnabas started a little church. Later they visited again, to encourage these new believers.

Paul and
Barnabas
worked as
missionaries,
taking the
good news to
people in other
countries.

Earthquake!

Paul also took a friend named Silas on his journeys.

At a town called Philippi, people became angry about their preaching. Officials had Paul and Silas beaten and thrown into jail. There they spent the night praying and singing.

About midnight an earthquake hit the prison. Doors flew open, and the prisoners' chains fell off.

When the jailer saw the prison gates wide open, he thought his prisoners had escaped. He would be in trouble for letting them get away, so he picked up his sword to kill himself.

"Don't harm yourself!" Paul called to him. "We're all here!"

The jailer fell down before Paul and Silas.

"What can I do to be saved?" he asked.

Paul and Silas said, "Believe on the Lord Jesus and you will be saved."

Acts 16:31 NLT

After he trusted Jesus, the jailer was baptized.

393

No work!

Story
361

*So the Lord's
message spread
and became
even more
powerful.*

Acts 19:20 CEV

Paul went to
the synagogue
in Ephesus and
told the Jews
about Jesus.

Paul preached at a great city called Ephesus.
Many people there started to believe in Jesus.

People in Ephesus used to worship the goddess
Diana. They bought silver statues of her to pray to at
home. But when people became Christians, they no
longer wanted these little statues.

Now the craftsmen who made these statues of Diana
had no work.

"We're losing money because of Paul's preaching,"
they said. "Let's get rid of him."

Riot!

A lot of people
in this riot
didn't even
know why they
were there!

So the statue-makers
started a riot.

"Diana is great!" they shouted.

"Let's get Paul and his friends!"

"This riot will cause trouble
for *all* of us!" said the mayor.
"Everyone, calm down, and go home."

The riot stopped. Paul was able to
leave the city safely.

To Rome

After many travels, Paul returned to Jerusalem. Roman soldiers arrested him there, in the Temple.

"Paul is a troublemaker," the high priest told the Roman ruler, Festus.

"Do you want to be judged in Jerusalem?" Festus asked Paul.

"No!" Paul said. "I am a Roman. I have the right to be tried by the Roman emperor, Caesar."

So Festus sent Paul to the great city of Rome for trial.

What happened to Paul in Rome?

Storm at sea

Soon Paul was on his way to Rome by ship. Before long, dark storm clouds appeared.

It was the wrong time of year to be making a long voyage. But the captain sailed on.

The storm got fiercer, and the wind blew the ship far off course. For many days the crew fought hard to stop the ship from sinking.

An angel appeared to Paul.

"God will protect everyone on board your ship," the angel told him.

Paul stood up and told the men... "God will save the lives of everyone on the ship."

Acts 27:21, 24
CEV

Did the angel's promise come true?

Shipwrecked

Story
365

I have faced danger in the cities, in the deserts, and on the stormy seas.

2 Corinthians 11:26 NLT

Sick people on the island came to Paul and asked him to heal them.

After two weeks, they saw an island. Great waves soon drove Paul's ship onto rocks. The boat started to tear apart.

But everyone reached shore safely, as God had promised Paul. They lit a fire on the beach to warm themselves. Paul helped gather firewood.

Suddenly, a snake slithered out from the sticks and bit Paul.

"He must be very wicked!" people cried. "He was saved from the shipwreck – but now he's been poisoned by this snake."

Paul held out his arm and shook off the snake. He was quite unharmed. God had looked after him again.

Story
366

Paul welcomed all who visited him... teaching about the Lord Jesus Christ.

Acts 28:30–31
NLT

We think Caesar executed Paul in Rome because Paul trusted in Jesus.

Rome at last!

Next spring the captain found another ship. They could now continue the voyage to Rome.

At last they landed in Italy. Soldiers marched the prisoners to the city of Rome.

Some followers of Jesus who lived in Rome came to welcome Paul.

Paul lived in Rome for two years. But he wasn't allowed to leave his house. Guards watched him all the time. But he never stopped telling people the good news about Jesus.